MW00637222

The Oilman's Daughter

The Oilman's Daughter

Jane Wilson Sheppard

Edited by Sally J. Bright

© Copyright 2016, Sally J. Bright Trust

All Rights Reserved.

No part of this book may be reproduced, stored in a retrieval system, or transmitted by any means, electronic, mechanical, photocopying, recording, or otherwise, without written permission from the author.

ISBN: 978-1-942451-41-9
eBook ISBN: 978-1-942451-50-1

YorkshirePublishing
www.yorkshirepublishing.com
Write Now.

For Jane's Family

Who Was Jane?

My mother, Jane Wilson Sheppard, was three years old in 1917 when her family moved to Oklahoma. Around seventy years later, she began writing anecdotes from her life. As I read stories of her childhood, I realized how much history she included—history that should be shared and preserved. She wrote about early oil fields and county fairs; Tulsa's landmarks, its race riot, and its riverside area; Oklahoma's 101 Ranch and Pawnee Bill; and her life inside a convent school.

Most of her memories revolve around her Tulsa neighborhood near the Arkansas River and her "interesting" family, as one neighbor euphemistically described it. She and her two younger nephews Billy and Jack had adventures ranging from poignant to hilarious. They were tended by black servants almost as though the family lived in the Deep South.

Jane was born in the family's Huntington mansion, Kenwood, which is still a showplace. Her father, John A. Sheppard, was a prominent attorney, landowner, and former state senator who came west with the early oil boom. He helped develop the Boynton Pool near Muskogee and by 1917 had settled his wife, Lydia; her mother; and Jane in Muskogee. Two older daughters, Edwina and Pauline, were married. The third, Wells, was in boarding school. By 1920, the family had moved to the fashionable new Buena Vista neighborhood in Tulsa near what Jane considered her forest along the Arkansas River.

As Jane's three sisters moved into and out of her life, an undercurrent of dysfunction gradually swept her from the security of childhood in surprising directions.

I edited and rearranged her material more or less chronologically, and I changed two names, but the memories and the naïve child's voice are hers. She begins with the train trip west—our first glimpse into a bygone era.

Sally J. Bright
March, 2016

Kenwood, Huntington, West Virginia
Photo Credit: Huntington Quarterly, Huntington, WV

Pauline, Edwina, Jane, Lydia and Wells
at Kenwood 1917

John A. Holding Baby Jane at Kenwood

A Brave New World

When we left Kenwood, I was lifted up the steps of a train. Mother took my hand, and we followed a porter down a narrow hallway. We reached our compartment, and he put our bags on a shelf over our heads. I was told to sit by the window. I heard a voice call, "All aboard!" over and over until only an echo of the sound remained. The train jerked forward, and we left the station.

Mother said we had to dress for dinner. She told me it was dangerous to go to the dining car. We would have to pass through cars and step outside between them. She said there were canopies over the walkways. We went to the end of the first car, opened a door, and stepped out. I could feel a rocking motion and hear wheels rolling beneath us. We stagger-walked. People in the day cars sat together without any room around them. They had shoe boxes of food, and children were eating bananas and apples. I wanted to stay with them.

Finally, we came to the dining room. Grandmother was already seated. Silver and crystal gleamed on the white tablecloths. I watched glasses rock back and forth to the rhythm of the train. I stuck my fingers in the finger bowl. I had to give that up. I wanted the white ruffle on the mignon, but they shook their heads. So I just watched waiters go from table to table.

As we went back, we saw people in the day car asleep, sprawled all over each other. In our compartment, the seats had disappeared. Instead there were beds with white sheets and large white pillows. Tiny lights shone. I thought it magic to lie in the dark and listen to train sounds. I heard whistles far away or close by when another train rushed by. I thought we would be on one of those returning to Kenwood soon.

The next day I heard the conductor calling, "Sant Looee" over and over. Mother was crying. Grandmother joined us, took my hand, and we stepped into the passageway. A porter brushed our coats. Grandmother tipped him, and we were helped off the train. Grandmother told Mother to quit crying, that soon she would be with John A.

In Oklahoma we first lived in the Severs Hotel in Muskogee. I spent most days in a room next to Grandmother's. In the mornings, a maid appeared with a tray of hot chocolate, toast, and cereal for me. Grandmother always called out telling me to eat my toast. I ate the center of the bread, then crawled under the bed and put the crusts up in the springs. In afternoons a white chauffeur took me down to the side yard of the hotel, where I could sit and pick clover. He told me to look for one with four leaves. I loved the hotel's red-leafed cannas that grew on each side of the walk. When I went back upstairs, Grandmother would be sitting in a large mahogany rocker, playing her wind-up Victrola and singing with Harry Lauder.

One morning I heard another voice in Grandmother's room. It was my sister Pauline—I called her Pawnee—and her new husband, Mike Fanning. The long days were over. I waited every morning for her voice to call me. "Jinsey," she would say, "Get out of that bed. We are going out." What joy!

One day we went downtown to Father's office. He seldom spoke to me, and I do not remember seeing him often in Muskogee, only when he drove us to Tulsa. But this day I sat at his desk in his large oak chair. The walls had cases of law books along with jars of earth in different colors. Some held Wilcox sand and rock cores with oil on them. Near a box of shale was a doodle-bug—a metal cone shape held by leather straps. A man would walk about the earth and hold this in front of him. If it swung around, or doodled, he would find oil. Mike said that was pure nonsense.

I heard Father tell Pawnee and Mike that he would drive around and look for a rising of the earth and then a slanting of the earth. He said it was a fault, and that was where he thought oil was. They laughed about the time he drove his new Model T out to look for a fault. He had spent most of his life on a horse riding the circuit court, so he always pulled back on the steering wheel to stop the car like he stopped a horse. He got out of the car without putting the brake on, and it rolled down a hill into a ravine. He had a long walk back. Then he bought the Stutz Bearcat. I sat listening to them, wishing I could have all the colored pencils on the desk.

When we returned to the hotel, Grandmother was singing with Caruso. I told her I had seen colored pencils and paper at the office, and I wanted them. She said she would have Duncan bring us some. Duncan was Father's bookkeeper. He sat in the corner of the office. Pawnee said that when he went on a bat, no one knew where anything was because most of it was in his head. He had a small mousy wife. She and Mother used to whisper to each other.

Sometimes Mike drove us to Tulsa to a grand place, the Tulsa Hotel. Oil men stood around the lobby or sat in Morris chairs, swapping leases. They wore what my Father wore now—corduroy jackets and pants and high lace-up boots. Mike said these men had found a new frontier. They came from many eastern places, mostly Kentucky and Virginia. They had thrown off all pretenses of formality, escaped the routines of the east, and begun a new life. I could see just their legs and boots and some skirts as we walked through the lobby.

We went into a small room that had a soda fountain, cigars, and all sorts of good-smelling drinks. We had chocolate sodas. They put me on the countertop and slipped cigar wrappings on my fingers. Pawnee bought me a small purse like hers. It had a looking glass on the bottom and two draw-strings to go over my arm. I felt very important when I carried it. The Tulsa Hotel had rugs with repeated patterns. When we walked very fast across them, I got dizzy.

The Severs lobby in Muskogee had marble floors and large pots of ferns. It was very pretty. The dining room was black and white, with white table-cloths and black chairs. Waiters wore black pants and white coats. Captain John, a large black man, was in charge of the dining room. He always came around to every table and asked if we liked our meal. People would just nod or mumble a nice platitude.

One evening he came to our table before we ordered, and Pawnee asked him what they were serving. Captain John said, "We is having Chicken La La King." My sister put the menu up to her face to hide her laugh. She was always finding funny things for our private jokes. Later Captain John wheeled a tea cart of wonderful desserts from table to table. My nose was on the pastry level. I caught all the sweet smells in one breath, but I always chose apple pie.

Often after breakfast we drove out to see Father's oil wells. The car bounced over narrow trails across fields. The ground around wells was clear, so we could walk right up to them. I could see tall wooden structures and hear pumping sounds. Thar-rump, thar-rump. Out a little way from the well was the boiler house with a large wooden wheel that had a belt on it. This made the well tool go up and down into the deep earth and hit the sides of the hole with a singing sound. That sound went through my body as I stood on the platform. Past the boiler house was a slush pit, a small pond with dark oil and chemicals from the well. A place of many colors.

The men who made all this happen were called drillers, riggers, or roughnecks. They had a different way of speaking and never talked to us, only to Father. I'm sure they knew from our clothes we were Easterners. Once when Mike was up on a platform wearing a light tan corduroy suit, something went wrong and black oil sprayed all over him. He raised his hands and acted like he was dancing. We could see him laughing and the men watching him. Then they began to laugh. Soon they were shaking hands with him. He took off his wristwatch, and the men passed it around and held it to their ears. They had never seen one. Later he explained to us that he told them he was glad to be with them and the accident was his luck of the Irish. Good things would happen to the well. After that they started waving at us when we visited.

A later trip gave us a different experience. We had driven out to see a new well Father was drilling. Pawnee told me to go with Mike, so I followed him to the well. I heard cables whining and the sound of the bit grinding into the earth. The same sound as the other well. As we stood there, the sound changed to a roar. The belt at the wheelhouse snapped and waved in the air like a flag. The men yelled, "Run! Run! She's coming up!" I felt the terror of it all.

But Father was so happy. He stood there throwing his cap in the air yelling, "Whooie! Whooie!" as black oil rained down on him.

I jumped off the platform and crawled under a fence into a grassy field. The long drill and bit came up out of the ground and swung around hitting things. Clang! Bang! Clang! And then it fell with a final sound. I crawled into the grass to hide. Insects clicked all around me. I felt warm and safe. I said, "I will stay here. I will not go back." I peeked out of my grass nest and saw a large mound of hay not far from me. I went to climb it.

Then I saw her. I knew her name—Doe Doe. She said, "Hello" and told me she lived in the haystack. I could hear Mike calling me. Then I saw him walking across the field. He did not see Doe Doe. He told me to go with him. I explained that I wanted to stay there and live with Doe Doe. He said she could come home with us. He carried me back to the car while Doe Doe walked beside him. He told Pawnee about her, and she said, "You can sit on my lap and she can sit beside us." I sat on Pawnee's lap all the way back to the hotel.

Doe Doe lived with us the rest of the year. When we went to New York, she left. My sister said she ran away to be on the stage, and she liked the bright lights. I never believed that. I think she went back to her haystack.

Pawnee said she wanted to "take in the sights." We spent one morning at Muskogee's county fair. She entered me in the "Best-Looking Child" contest and I won a ribbon. Mother was furious when she found out. She said it was very common. I didn't care, and I didn't understand why she was upset.

Later Father found a house for us and we moved. It was a bungalow on Thirteenth Street that Mother called our "little gray cottage in the West." She met other women and they had clubs and teas and played bridge. They decided that Tulsa was a more social town. It would be more interesting, and they could have nice houses built.

But I liked living in Muskogee. I liked to go see Mrs. Hancock. She had a large old house right downtown. We sat in her parlor and sipped tea. I did not like the horsehair material on the chairs, but I loved to hear her talk. She pulled the words apart in a Virginia way of speaking. I missed that sound when we came west, and I found it again in her voice. She was nearly blind, Grandmother said. When she wanted to go someplace, she stood in the road outside her house. Someone would pick her up. Pawnee said her daughter was married into the tobacco millions.

Jane and Grandmother

Wherever we went, we wore white gloves we bought from twin sisters. They had us sit at the counter in their store, put an elbow on it, and hold one hand up. They carefully pulled soft kid gloves over our fingers. Fitting gloves always gave us time to talk about recent events.

My sister Wells left school in the east after she found out Pawnee and Mike were with us. She made many demands, including her own place to live. She decided to show Mother that she was her own boss. She stayed out all night in a canoe on the lake with a boy. Everyone was upset with her. Grandmother said, "What will people think about us!" She also said she saw Wells making eyes at Mike. Wells found an apartment across the hall from Pawnee and Mike's. Pawnee kept me away from her, and when we moved to Tulsa I found out why. By then Pawnee and Mike had moved to New York.

Wells, Edwina, Jane, Pauline 1918

Mother told me we were going to Tulsa because she wanted to look at some houses. Everyone was doing that. Father would drive us because Roy was still away in the war. The trip was to be an all-day affair, so she packed extra clothes. I was put in the back seat. I sat, then stood up to see outside. I saw a river and a lot of white sand with trees along the side. I wanted to get out and run across the sand. It was hard to stay in the back seat for such a long time.

Gradually the car turned away from the river and around the side of a hill. A storm spread over us, and rain began. Lightning flashed all around the car. A gray haze covered the view. The car began to slide around and then stopped.

Mother, in a strange voice, said, "Jack."

Father said, "Now, Dutch. I have to go down the road and find us some help."

I curled up in the back seat and hid my head. After a long time he returned. The rain stopped, and I listened to the music of thunder gradually echo away from us. Then voices. I stood up on the seat so I could see past the front window. There was a man with two large animals. The car lights gave me a better look. He was carrying a chain. Then he put it on our car.

I heard him whistle and talk to the animals. The car lurched forward. I fell backward, then scrambled to my feet so I could see the animals. They pulled us down the road. When they stopped, Father came back and we drove to Tulsa.

"They were fine mules," he said. "Much better than an automobile."

One day Roy Green returned to us from the war. Mother told us that when he came to the door she said, "Oh, Roy, we thought you were dead."

He said, "I have come a long way to be back with my family."

We were all so happy. Father had brought Roy to Kenwood when he was very young. He learned to be our houseman, yardman, and chauffeur. The day he returned, he drove us to Agency Hill. Hills were all around Muskogee, and that was the tallest. It had a water tower. I think there was a memorial to veterans of the war too. Another place Roy drove us was a park. And he drove us all around town where trees made archways over streets, and rows of white houses had large front porches.

Grandmother said, "Isn't this just grand."

"Yessum," Roy said.

Lydia and Jane, Muskogee Water Tower 1919

The New Home

Father bought the Tulsa house my mother wanted at 1904 South Cheyenne. Frank Lippa had been building it for himself, but with Father's generous offer, he sold it. It would not be finished for several months.

Now Roy could drive us to Tulsa. We did not use the sandy, muddy river road. We took the road by towns named Boynton and Mounds. Mounds had a bank right on a corner. My parents said it was a fine, safe building. I liked the way its sandstone came to a point.

We went to the new house every week. I saw wooden floors, swinging doors to push back and forth, and stairs to run up and down. Sometimes we also went to the Tulsa Hotel. Men still stood in the lobby trading. Oil was forty cents a barrel, but sometimes they sold it for twenty.

I learned that they called Indian deals blanket leases. With their lease money, Indians bought large cars and ambulances to ride around in. Their land was changed forever. Wooden oil wells stood row upon row. Then flat prairies became fields of pumping jacks going up and down. Drilling rods made strange squeaking sounds in rhythm. The odor of oil and gas was everywhere. At night the prairie lit up with gas flares burning red flames.

Finally we moved when the furniture from Kenwood arrived. Six men carried the large tan marble altar into the front hall. On either side, they placed the bronze Italian lamps. Mother hired Mayo Furniture to make blue velvet draperies for the living room first, then other colors for all the rooms. Bookcases were built in because we would not have a library. Now oil men were coming to our house to talk about rigs and leases and gushers and dry holes.

Roy found a nice woman named Lena to work for us. He was so pleased with his spacious quarters over our garage. He liked Tulsa, especially the section north of town called Greenwood, where there were Negro businesses. All around our house, he made flower beds. He planted pink peonies along the south side of the living room. He filled our back yard with dark red plum trees that flowered white in the spring. He planted rows of grapes on a low fence to separate our house from the one south of us. That was the last house on our side of the block.

The New Home 1980's

Upstairs in 1920 by Jane

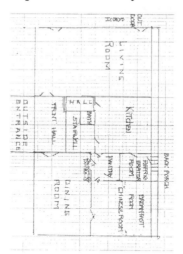

Downstairs in 1920 by Jane

Later Roy cleared the land between our garage and the river road. He did not clear it like the front yard but just took out the old brush. He said he was finding snakes and getting rid of them. He was also digging a cave where I could play. I liked to walk down there and watch him work in the sandy earth. If I walked closer to the river, I could see what was floating by. The pools of shiny oil with blue and gold streaks formed circles then uncoiled and floated downstream.

Across the river, they built a large refinery for the oil. Acres of enormous white metal tanks held surplus oil. We could see them from the south bedroom. If a tank caught fire, the refinery blew a whistle that could be heard for many miles. After the whistle blew, short blasts told which tank it was. You counted the blasts. Tank five, five blasts. I would run upstairs and look across the river. The oil turned into red flames going into the sky, with black smoke curling around them.

A fire was an event. When women heard the whistles and blasts, they went to the alcoves where they had telephones on little tables. First they picked up something that resembled a black lamp without a shade. They held it in their left hands, then with their right hands they lifted the black receiver shaped like a small bottle with a flared end. This they held to their ears. Then they said, "The refinery is on fire!"

Women in Tulsa began driving cars. Mother had a dealer bring her an electric model. I thought it was the ugliest thing I had ever seen. It was square, with glass windows on the upper sides of the doors and at the back. It was like a very old carriage without horses. The four wheels were turned by a metal rod that came from the left side of the driver's seat. There it was, just a box, and it did not have the wonderful sound of a motor. So I sat in it while Mother steered us up the street. I saw Father turning and roaring around the corner in his Stutz Bearcat ahead of us. Mother honked the funny sounding horn, but Father went speeding by. He did not know she could drive, so he did not think to wave. She was furious and sent the car back. Harry Botham sent us a Willys after that.

We soon considered Lena a dear servant. She was always there. On hot summer days, she closed the downstairs drapes before noon and set the big Emerson fans in motion. In evenings she opened the drapes and the windows so the cool air made the house comfortable again.

One day she told me I should go upstairs and see my sister Wells. She had left Muskogee and moved into the new house. I walked into her room and said, "Hello."

She said, "Get out, and don't you ever come into my room again."

If I was in the bathroom, she dragged me out. If I was on the staircase, she tried to trip me. She came into my room and pushed me against the wall. I became fearful and began to walk in my sleep. Lena kept awakening me. Grandmother spoke to Mother about it, and she took me to a doctor. He said I needed more exercise. I was sent to ballet classes. Then I found the woods and the barn along the river. They set me free, away from such anger.

One summer day, my oldest sister, Edwina, came from Illinois with her two sons. When I heard a car door close, I went to my bedroom window to watch them. I was in there because I had the measles. Mother had given me a red scooter. I was wheeling it around the room when I heard a knock at my door.

I opened it and saw the two boys. The taller one had brown hair and brown eyes like mine. He was dressed in khaki shorts and a buttoned shirt. The other one was smaller, with lighter hair and brown eyes. The tall one said, "Hello. My name is Bill, and we have come to stay with you for a while." I stood looking at them with my hands on the handlebars.

Bill said, "Let us in."

"I can't. I have the measles."

"What do you have there?"

I told them about the gift I got because I was sick. He said, "Since you are unable to come out, you should give it to us."

"No. This is my scooter!"

I wished he would go away. He yelled, "Do you know what it means to be selfish?"

Again, I shook my head, more determined to keep my scooter. "It means you keep everything for yourself and never help anyone. You must share with us." He pushed open the door, grabbed the handlebars of my scooter, and wheeled it out into the hall. I sat on the floor and cried.

As time went by, I became used to them. Edwina and her husband, Pep, often left the boys with us. We had breakfast together in the kitchen on the large white wicker table. Lena served us pancakes. Sometimes Grandmother came downstairs and sat with us. She poured half her coffee into a saucer and gave me the other half in the cup. She called the boys the Katzenjammers after a newspaper comic strip. She would not allow them in her room.

After breakfast, if Edwina was with them, Billy always called to her, "Ed, honey. Ed, honey."

She immediately appeared with a book for him. She was teaching him Latin. Jack and I usually went out of the west porch door to play or at first to watch men digging the hole for our swimming pool. It was fun to climb on the dirt mounds. Sometimes Billy followed us out but stayed on the porch. He leaned over the black iron railing, held his book in the air, and loudly read, "*Amo, amas, amat.*"

Lydia, Jane and John A.

John A. and Jane with Julia's House in Background

18

When our swimming pool was finished, Mother bought water wings for me. They were two gray cloth bags filled with air that she tied to my shoulders. In afternoons I climbed down the ladder and paddled around. Or if I held very still, the large frog that lived there would climb on one of my wings.

One day I had been in the water a short time when I saw my sister Wells and her new friend come out the side door and sit in the swing by the pool. Grandmother had told me they were sparking. Wells motioned for me to come over and meet him. She told me his name was Tom.

I said, "Hello."

He asked, "How old are you?"

"I am six."

"Oh, did you say you were sick? Ha, ha."

I just stood there, dripping wet. I repeated, "I am six."

"Well, if you are sick, here—take a puff of my pipe."

I felt awkward and did not understand.

My sister said, "Try it."

I took the pipe, sucked on it, and began coughing.

"Ha, ha."

My mouth felt terrible. I ran into the house.

That fall, Pawnee and her little boy named Sonny came for a visit. Mother was giving her and Wells and me a sewing lesson in the large upstairs room. When she explained a six-gore skirt, I pinned mine together wrong. Wells made fun of me.

Mammy (Sonny's Nurse) and Jane

Mother stopped that by asking if we would like to see her memory trunk. This was always a special occasion. To us she was the symbol of love and beauty. She never told us what to do. She never corrected us. But we knew "they" were in charge. Their routines gave us a sense of direction.

She opened the large brass clasps in the center of an upright trunk. One side had a closet for hanging gowns, and the other side had small and large drawers. She brought out beautiful things, explaining each. "Here is an ostrich feather fan that I wore to President Taft's ball." Its handle was carved tortoise shell. She passed her jewelry to Pauline and Wells, and they put on the Majolica beads, the gold snake necklace with emerald eyes, and the black pearls. Then they tried on coral cameos, diamond bracelets, a long diamond brooch, and the little finger ring. It had twenty-eight diamonds that spiraled into an opal at the top. Sonny tried to look through the pearl-handled opera glasses.

Lydia

Lydia Dressed for President Taft's Ball

Out of another drawer she brought family portraits with old velvet mats in gold frames and wooden carved outer frames. Some were hinged in a set of three. People in the pictures stood by a balustrade or sat, always staring straight ahead, not smiling. They looked like Grandmother's doll, Fanchion.

As Mother lifted out the gowns, we three stood and held them in front of ourselves. Some were velvet with taffeta ruffles. One was black satin, with hand-sewn sequins all over it. One pale blue dress had pearls on the front and shoulders. I liked the white lace one that draped with rows of ruffles around the skirt. I wanted to keep the bright pink embroidered Spanish shawl.

At last, she showed us the secret compartment at the bottom of the trunk. It held a silver flask wrapped in blue cloth. We asked if we could hide things in there. "No," she said.

Then she told us where she wore the beautiful gowns—and stories of trips to Chautauqua, Atlantic City, Virginia Beach, Larchmont, and the exciting trip to Florida. She showed us pictures of Aunt Cass there, with her outdoor summer kitchen, and pictures of Grandmother when she was young. They drove a large automobile up and down Daytona Beach, a beautiful deserted place by the ocean.

John A., Pauline, Lydia, Edwina

22

Grandmother also had a large floor trunk. It sat in the corner of her bedroom where she spent her time reading and lying in bed. I sat on her bed when she got out her scrapbook full of postcards from places she had visited. She opened it only for me. I turned the pages as she told me about each one. I knew we would soon come to the card with real fur from a black bear. I loved to pet it. Between the scrapbook pages she had Confederate money. She said it was not worth a tinker's damn. She had a horsehair snare she said the sister of Jeff Davis gave her. He used it to catch fish. She also had one of his umbrella handles with a carved bulldog head and golden glass eyes. And she had a hand-carved wooden box filled with yellowed newspaper clippings of Edgar Guest poetry that she read to me. It was our secret.

Grandmother kept money under a brick of the fireplace in her room. Her son Will sent it to her every month. No one but me knew about it—another secret.

June 1921

This June morning I awakened and dressed and opened the door to my room. The house was so quiet that I thought it must be very early. I wanted to spend the day outdoors, so I walked into the hall that led to the stairs. Grandmother's door was closed, but I heard her canary singing

Lena always fixed my breakfast, but she was not in the kitchen. I began walking through the house looking for her. I pushed the swinging doors of the pantry and went into the dining room. "Lena," I called. She did not answer. I walked across the front hall to the French doors of the living room. They were closed. I opened one and looked in.

Father stood in front of the fireplace. Mother sat in the wingback chair beside him. I caught my breath and wondered why they were there and why they looked upset. Mother told me to go back upstairs. Instead I went to the basement door and down five steps to the landing. Lena sometimes cooked in the two fireless cookers kept there. I turned right and went down four more stairs to the wood room. The hall to the right went to the wine cellar. I turned left to where Lena lived.

"Lena," I called, and pushed her door open. Her room was full of Negroes. They sat on the floor and on her bed or just stood.

Lena shut the door behind me and said, "Miz Jane, we has got troubles and they has to hide. Jes don't tell a soul."

A small dark girl stood beside her. Lena said, "This is Gertrude." Neither of us spoke.

Then we went upstairs and Lena cooked my breakfast while Gertrude stood beside the table watching me. Lena fixed Grandmother's tray for me to take and told me not to go outside all day.

"Why? Why do you say that?"

"Ask your grandmother why." She waved her hand at me as they disappeared into the basement.

Grandmother was sitting in her rocking chair by the three south windows so she could see the river. She thought it was important to look at a river.

I asked, "Mawee, why can't I go out today?" as I put the tray on her lap. She picked up her coffee cup and drank slowly.

"They are killing darkies out there. You cannot be any part of it."

She dipped her bread in the bowl of sorghum and butter then put it in her mouth. I waited, staring at her dark brown eyes, her grey hair piled on top of her head, knowing the bond between us.

"Those crazy men called KKK are shooting at everything that moves."

Now the whole day was spoiled, and I was unhappy.

As I started downstairs I heard a knock on the door. I crawled back up. When Mother opened the door, five men entered. They wore white robes and carried guns. She led them into the living room and closed the French doors. I heard a "Pssst" from the upper balcony. It was Grandmother. She told me to slip out the back and go listen to what they said. I went down the stairs, out the kitchen door, and crawled under the living room window. I could peek in and see my father standing by the fireplace. I could tell who some of the men were by their shoes and voices.

They were talking about going to Greenwood and seeing what they could do. They were all in a club together. I had heard Roy and Lena talk about them.

The man who lived at the end of the block said loudly, "John A., we had a meeting last night. We are going to get in our cars today and go after them."

Another man said, "We want to know what you are going to do about this."

Father bowed his head and put his hands behind his back. He finally answered, "My ancestors freed their slaves, and I am not going to hurt or kill anyone's servant." Then he brought his right hand around and put it across his heart and said in a loud voice, "The law is the law and shall be abided by."

The man that lived in the middle of the block said, "You must be one of those Nigger lovers from Virginia."

Father quietly said, "No, I am a lawyer."

"Let's not waste any more time here," the loud man said. They began leaving.

I realized I was supposed to be upstairs, so I ran back to the kitchen. Mother was there. She told me not to say a word about the people in the basement and not to go outside. She called down to Lena to cook for all of them.

Lena told me later that Gertrude's mother had been killed. Boots and Napoleon had found her and brought her and their fox terrier named Tuts with them. The couple stayed with us for a while, but Gertrude lived with Lena in the basement for years.

Roy eventually told me he had brought the Negroes down a path along the river. That was the way he used to get our fresh milk from a farm near the bridge. Later people called it the Eleventh Street Bridge.

School Days

E very Sunday, Mother and I went downtown to Mass at Holy Family. The church had opened a school before we moved to Tulsa, so I started first grade there. In the mornings, Roy or my father drove me. Roy usually picked me up afterward.

I cried a lot when I was sent to Conway Bruin, a school on the north side of Tulsa. My parents learned that girls of good families were going there. It had no art classes, only programs for showing off talent. My June Runyan dance lessons helped me take part. In one class, we read a book about a beggar who became a prince. The teachers planned a play about part of it, and they needed a screen to make the room look like a stage. I asked if I could copy *The Blue Boy* on the screen. All went well. The algebra teacher asked me to do her picture.

The headmistress of Conway Bruin closed it because of poor health, so all of us moved to Holland Hall in a red brick building on South Boulder. This was very convenient for me because it was only two blocks from home. There we studied knights in armor. At our house, I found pens and inks and made some drawings of the knights for our school room. Grandmother was very impressed. Mother did not seem interested. I saved all the pictures for Pawnee's visits.

Now that my school was so close, I could visit the neighborhood barn before classes started. The barn was below the long row of houses on the east side of Cheyenne by a creek that ran into the river. To get there, I walked across the street and up a driveway where purple violets grew in great clusters. There was a wall on the north side of their garage. I could jump from it to the dirt alley that went down to the end of the block. Then another dirt road ran east. When I came to the paddock fence, it was easy to pull myself over and walk into the back of the barn. Johnny, the stableman, always said, "Halloo."

Neighbors owned all the horses in the ten stalls except for one, a black stallion named LaFrance. He kicked the stall and neighed and circled his area most of the time. Johnny and his father told me not to climb on that gate. I stood across the aisle and watched him. He was wonderful. Then I ran to the wooden feedboxes and got two handfuls of bran. Mabel, the sorrel horse in the last stall on the right, waited for me. We ate bran together.

One day Johnny said, "Come down early Saturday. We will hitch the sulky and go to the river." Oh, I could hardly wait.

When Saturday finally came, I went to the barn very early. Johnny had the sulky ready and pulled me up onto the black wooden seat. There was little room, but I squeezed in. The horse tossed her head and danced. I held on to the seat. We began trotting down the dirt road toward the river. Johnny held the reins with both hands and made clicking noises. The horse moved with a long walking gait as we rolled along the river road. A gray mist hovered over the water. Trees stood like tall giants. Spider webs on the wild grapevines twinkled with crystal lights. The sun began to rise from the earth. A brown rabbit ran ahead of us, then stopped and watched us go by.

"Take the reins," Johnny said as he moved over. I sat upright and did what he said. "Put your feet on the board below and brace them."

I felt the rhythm of the horse. Johnny began to sing an Irish song, and I knew this was the most wonderful day of my life. When we returned, Johnny's father gave me a large cup of hot coffee and they told me stories of horse races. I thanked them for a nice ride, left by the east door, and walked to the nearby creek.

It ran over large flat rocks on the river road. This was a wagon crossing, and cars went over it too. I waded across the rocks, turned left, and walked along the bank of the creek toward the river. I saw empty shells of crawfish that raccoons had been eating, tiny mouse tracks, and a long dented line of a snake in the mud. Green plants grew around the bank. Many small movements below made the water ripple. Snails clung to rocks as water passed over them. I glimpsed a large turtle on the bottom. Then I heard the waterfall and turned toward the thicket.

The tall weeds were still gray from winter past. I stooped over and stepped carefully along a small animal path that wound around rocks and old stumps, ending in the secret forest.

I stepped out on the soft black dirt and old leaves. Tiny sprouts of grass came up through the leaves. I stood quietly looking at the large beautiful trees. I believed elves lived here, guarding the Chinese box I kept in an oak tree near the waterfall. In it I had a crystal rock that sparkled in the sunlight, a gold ring, one pearl, and a picture of my favorite sister. No one could open it because they would not know what piece of bamboo to push.

To reach it, I would swing up on the lower branch of the mulberry tree, climb it, then step over to the oak. In its fork was an opening where I kept the box. I took it out, climbed down, and went to a special place where moss grew on a large rock. After picking off twigs and leaves, I opened my box and laid out all the treasures. Then I went to the log near the waterfall and watched things come down the creek over the falls. I collected tassels from the oak trees to put in the tree where my box stayed. I collected walnuts because Lena liked them. When I came back from the waterfall, I sat and looked up at a wonderful old cottonwood tree. It was the time of day when birds are quiet. I leaned back on the moss and fell asleep.

A squirrel ran down the trunk and barked at me until I awakened. Sunlight was coming in from the west. I quickly returned my treasures to their box. Then I realized I had forgotten to bring the coral bead I found in sand near our well.

Perhaps, I thought, I could run in from the north side of the forest on a school morning and bring the bead. With this in mind I slowly walked home.

Monday morning I left the house very early. I ran down the driveway past the violets, jumped the wall, and went east across the school parking lot. From there I climbed down an embankment and walked a pipe across a small green pond. Frogs croaked and jumped as I passed. I put the coral in my box alongside the other treasures. As I hurried under the large cottonwood on the creek, I heard squirrels chattering. A very small one fell on its back by my feet. It did not move. I picked it up, put grass in my jacket pocket, and laid the little one in there. I said, "I will take you home at noon, and Lena will care for you." I buttoned the pocket and walked to school.

I opened the large front door, walked past offices, and climbed the stairs to my first class. When the bell rang for classes to change and I went into the hall, the headmistress was waiting. She pointed her finger at me and said, "I want to see you in my office."

When I entered, she was sitting at her large desk, frowning and looking very cross. She said, "Some of you have been bringing cigarettes to school and smoking in the restroom. I can see that you have a package in your right pocket. Empty it immediately!"

I stood there wondering what to do. Phyllis Isley smoked. Her governess let her do anything she wanted. She always had girls hanging around copying her. She said she was going to be a movie star.

Finally I reached in my pocket and felt the squirrel's tail. I pulled it out and put it on her desk. Wide awake, it jumped to the front of her dress and ran over her shoulder. She screamed and called me terrible names. The squirrel jumped up the curtain behind her. I ran around the desk and grabbed it by the back of the head, as Roy had taught me. I shoved the little one in my pocket with one hand while the other hand pushed doors open. I ran out of her office, out of the school, across the drive, over the embankment, and down into the forest. I turned him loose, and he scrambled up his tree, scolding me and jerking his tail. I stayed there till time to go home for dinner.

Mother said the headmistress had called her and claimed I had a varmint in my pocket. I explained how the little one fell out of the tree and about the cigarettes and that the headmistress called me bad names.

After dinner and after Lena had gone downstairs, I saw Gertrude standing behind the door motioning me to come with her. Lena and Roy were waiting in the basement. He said Mother had asked him to find me, so he wanted to know why I wasn't in school. I told them all about it except for the secret place I kept my treasure.

Lena rocked back and forth on her bed as I told the story, saying, "Uh huh" and "Lawsey."

When I finished, Roy said, "Yessah, that squirrel is the smartest squirrel in the woods. He done went to school."

Mother decided I should return to Holy Family for a while. Now I could use my roller skates to go home down sidewalks along Boulder. I had to carry my books and skates across Eleventh Street, but when I put them on I had a great time. Some sidewalks were buckled by the trees that lined and shaded Boulder. I knew where they were. When I reached Nineteenth, I turned right and coasted the hill to our house.

One day before I left school, Sister Gregory said, "Come with me."

I followed her to the front of the school, where she opened a door. I saw easels, paint brushes, and tables with painted china dishes on them. She took me to an easel by the north window that overlooked the church side entrance. "This will be your easel. You must work here every day and become a painter." She taught me mixtures and canvas work. Every day after school, I made copies of old masters. I painted them for my sister Pawnee.

Sketch by Jane

Spavinaw

As I sat at the kitchen table, I blew on the vase of pink peonies so more petals would fall. Lena had given me a bowl of hominy grits with an egg in its center. She walked back and forth from the stove to the refrigerator room. She always held her elbows against her hips. Her arms stuck out on either side and her hands hung down. Her wrists moved in tune with the shuffle of her body. It was a dance walk. She was frying chicken, so it was Sunday.

Roy brought the picnic basket up from the basement. Another sign of Sunday was that he wore his Army uniform. Father thought Roy honored his country this way.

He said, "Miz Jane, we is gwine drive to see a new lake today."

The wicker picnic basket had two large wooden handles that met in the center when it closed and lay on each side when it opened. Its base was metal, and so was the interior. Inside, a double leather case lined with velvet held thermos jugs. Another metal box held ice. Lena would pack the basket with the chicken, potato salad, salt rising bread, pound cake, and peaches. She put iced tea in the thermoses.

After breakfast, I hurried upstairs and dressed. Downstairs, Mother and Father sat in the living room. I followed Roy around. When he walked to the car, I walked to the car. When he put the basket in the trunk, I knew it was time. He put me in the seat by him and drove the car up to the front door. Father and Mother came out, and we began the drive.

After we left town, driving with the sun in our eyes, we saw large gray and white farm houses with porches all around. Black buggies sat in the front yards. Roy thought they were fine places. I pressed my face against

35

the glass to see the children playing, wishing they were closer so I could see their faces. They wore black hats and black clothes.

After many miles, the scenery changed. We drove up and over hills with pine trees everywhere. Small rocks covered the ground. We saw cabins back among the trees. Mother said they belonged to Indians, and Father said they had been moved out here by a man named Jackson. Their children had left everything outside that they should have put in their closets.

Finally, we were at the dam. A big sign showed the lake name, Spavinaw. Roy parked by a beautiful clear stream and helped all of us out of the car. Water from the dam fell over the spillway to run down the stream. We went up wide wooden stairs to the top of a mound. A beautiful blue lake lay before us as far as we could see. They said the water was going to Tulsa.

Roy returned to the car and wiped off the large headlights. He raised the front hood to look at the engine. Roy loved the Winton sedan. When we returned, he stood by the door as we got back into our seats. He pushed the button to start the motor. I felt it vibrate and waited for us to roll along.

We drove beside the stream, and Father told Roy to find a nice place for lunch. We parked by a grove of trees. Under one of the larger ones, Roy spread the braided rug Aunt Cass had sent from Florida. We sat down to enjoy our picnic. Roy served the plates and poured iced tea. As he handed me a glass, I motioned to the big black snake wrapped around a branch in the tree. He saw it and nodded.

Mother and Father were laughing and talking until a big black and orange and blue lizard ran across the blanket. Another one chased it. The snake dropped off the tree limb and landed in front of us. He was going to catch a lizard.

Mother screamed. Father picked her up and put her in the car. I moved backward toward the car, breathless, staring at the snake. I climbed on the running board and clung to the door. Roy had put a jack handle behind the picnic basket. He hit the snake and stomped his foot behind its head. He took a knife out of his pocket, cut the head off, and buried it with his trench shovel.

The lizards had disappeared. Roy pulled me from the running board and put me in the seat. Then he put our picnic basket and rug back in the car and we drove away silently.

After a few miles, Mother began to look for what was left in the basket. She passed food to us and tapped on the divided window to offer some to Roy. Soon she began laughing and said, "One of our neighbors told us they were going to build a large cabin by Spavinaw Lake." She finished, "They can have it, snakes and all!"

The Three Musketeers

Edwina and Pep were living in Tulsa for a season. That meant Billy and Jack were going to spend Christmas with us! When they came for dinner Christmas Eve, we three talked about Santa Claus and wondered what we would get the next day. We were sent to bed early.

I truly believed Santa was a real person. They told me he flew through the air with wonderful reindeer and a sleigh full of toys for everyone. This seemed right because at church they made me read things over and over that were like that. The Father, Son, and Holy Ghost were in the sky, and Santa was there too. Once I thought I had heard reindeer on the roof and tiny sounds of bells far away.

After breakfast Christmas morning, Mother rang the Chinese gong and we ran to the closed doors of the living room. When she opened them, we saw the most beautiful tree filled with lights, icicles, popcorn, and sparkling ornaments. My favorites were glass birds with long silk tails. Under the tree lay presents Santa had left. We were so happy.

Our Christmas dinner was at one in the afternoon. In the dining room, green garlands decorated the mahogany sideboard and the tall drums that stood on its sides. The center of the table had a display of Santa Claus sitting in his sleigh surrounded by snow and holly. He wore a red velvet suit trimmed with real white fur. He held reins that went to six deer with more fur. When Santa raised his arms, the reindeer moved their heads up and down.

Lena had set the table with the embroidered cloth from France, the white Haviland china, and the etched crystal glasses. Father was seated at the head and Mother at the foot, with the rest of us on opposite sides. Mother had a small wrapped gift at each plate. Mine was my first Indian bracelet. Lena and Roy brought our food, and the party was quite festive.

When Roy carried in the dessert tray, Lena placed each person's dish around the table. All of a sudden large coils of gray snakes began to grow under the reindeer's feet. I knew what they were—the snakes that coil and look terrible for Fourth of July. Pep laughed loudly, and Edwina shrieked with laughter. The furry reindeer, with their heads staring up at the ceiling, stood in piles of manure.

Jack looked across the table at me. He was crying.

Father said, "Roy, take the children to the breakfast room."

When the long day was over and I climbed into bed, there was a note on my pillow. It read, "There is no Santa Claus. Edwina."

Edwina and Pep moved back to Illinois, but they often sent the boys to us. One morning when Jack and I were in our back yard, he walked over to the small sidewalk against the quarters where Roy lived and said, "Let's go to the river."

We went down the steps from our yard to the sidewalk and garage under the quarters. Tall cement walls lined either side of the parking area. White wooden beams shaded it with hanging wisteria vines and their lavender flowers. We thought it looked like something Maxfield Parrish would draw. Roy always drove into this area. Then we got out and went up the steps to our house. Parking there was safer than parking at the front door because of the hill.

I followed Jack into the street. We turned left and walked down Nineteenth Street toward the river, but we were soon drawn to the new house built into the hillside across Nineteenth. We walked over and began climbing squares of sod. We had to stick our toes in between them to reach the top. There we saw the new stone house.

"Oh, what a beautiful house," I whispered.

"It does not stand up tall like yours."

"We should not be here."

But Jack walked into the yard, then waved his arm and called me to follow. I watched him step slowly. Then he ran back to me.

"It's a bear! A real live bear!"

I forgot to whisper and said in a loud voice, "A bear?"

We walked closer. The bear saw us and made funny snuffling noises. He stood up and walked the length of a chain attached to his collar.

Jack leaned closer and spoke to him. "Are you a woods bear or a Pooh bear?"

The bear put his arms out, and I thought he was such a wonderful creature that I walked into his arms and hugged his furry body.

Jack yelled, "Look out! Get away!"

I was so happy to be in a bear's arms that I ignored Jack. The bear hugged me. And then he hugged me more.

"Jack, he will not let me go!"

"Slip down to his feet."

I tried, but he still held me.

Jack said, "I will go get help."

After what seemed like a long time, I heard Jack behind me saying, "Banana! Banana for a nice bear."

The bear took his arms from me and reached for the banana. I crawled away then ran across the yard and the street into the woods behind the quarters. I sat in the tall grass and waited for Jack. I had felt the great power of the bear.

Later we found out that the man who owned the house had kept the bear for some Shriner activity.

One summer morning I was thinking about a train. I thought the front porch swing would make a nice train. I would play engineer. I went into the side yard to be sure no one was around. Then I climbed on the large wicker swing and stood on the end near the front of the house. I grabbed the chains and began to push the swing sideways. I stood on the arm and yelled, "Whoo! Whoo!" and my train began to leave the station.

Then I saw Pete crossing the street, walking toward me. That was strange, because he never played with us. He usually stayed in his house. I stopped the train.

"Hello," he said.

I said hello but did not want to.

He asked, "Where are your two cousins?" I did not tell him they were my nephews.

"They will be here next week." I wished he would leave. "I have an army tent I wanted them to see." He paused and added, "Would you like to see it?" He paused again. "You would like it. Come and see."

I wanted to drive my train, but I thought I could tell Billy and Jack about the army tent when they came.

"All right." I got down and followed him across the street.

We did not take any shortcuts or jump up on walls and walk on them as we went up Cheyenne. He just talked about his tent. It seemed like a long way because his white house was on the next corner from ours. It did not have any porches. I walked behind him around the north side to his back yard. I saw a dark green shape like a square block with a slanted top. The corners had poles. The door was cloth, of a sort. I wondered why anyone would want to live in that.

"Go inside," he said. I crawled in. The floor was just grass. A pole stood in the middle. Pete came behind me, and when I crawled near the pole, he grabbed my arms and tied me to it with clothesline rope. He yelled, "I have captured an Indian for the United States Army! You shall stay here, and the Army will decide what to do with you!"

"Untie me! Let me go!"

But he said I was a captive, and he left. The tent got very warm when the sun started shining on it. I sat and asked myself, Why did I come up here? Why do they capture Indians? Finally, I decided I was an Indian but no one had ever told me. I stared at the flap door of the tent. I could see him coming.

He sat on the ground in front of me holding two hard-boiled eggs. He slowly ate them. They smelled good, and I was thirsty. My fright turned to rage.

"I hate you!" I yelled. "You are a terrible person. I am going to tell everyone!"

"Ha! No one is home today, and who would believe you." He left.

I stared at the egg shells. Then my whole body filled with anger. I had never been so angry. I pushed up with my knees. I rocked back and forth. The pole wobbled. I pushed more, the pole went over, and I fell with the whole tent around me. I moved my arms up to the end of the pole then stood up with it on my back. When it slid down, I slipped my hands out and was soon untied. I raised the tent and ran from his yard into tall cane grass. I did not stop running until I reached the river road. When I saw the coffee bean tree, I knew where I was—the place where the butterflies slept.

Lena was in the kitchen when I finally returned home. She looked at me and asked, "Whar you been, Miz Jane? You look a sight."

I did not answer. I drank the milk she gave me. Then I said, "Lena, who are the Indians? Who is the Army? Why does the Army treat the Indians so badly?"

She had been padding her way across the kitchen. She stopped with her hands in midair and said, "I cannot talk to you about such things." She shook her head back and forth.

I told her what happened. I told her that now I knew I was an Indian. She laughed and said that could never be true.

When she put her arms around me, everything was all right again. She said she would not tell anyone but Roy. I went upstairs to get ready for dinner.

My train never left the station.

The next time Billy and Jack came, Roy had taken our sandbox away. There was just a little sand left under the mulberry tree. As we were running our hands through it, Billy demanded our attention, saying he had learned a new word. We stared, waiting.

Billy said, "Son of a bitch."

"What does that mean?" I asked.

"It means your mother was a dog."

"Why?" Jack asked.

"What do you mean, 'Why'? Listen to what I say!"

Jack asked, "Why would anyone want to say that?"

"Don't you get it, dummy? It is a bad word and you are supposed to use it when you are mad at another man."

Jack said, "You use it. I think it is dumb."

I felt it was terrible. I changed the subject with, "I must tell you what happened to me."

When I finished the Indian story, Billy reacted immediately. "Why did you go up that block we did not know anything about?"

"I wanted to see the tent and then tell you about it."

"We have to go up there and look it over. This is war!"

That evening we asked if we could sleep on pallets in the south yard. The night was warm, so they said we could. Moonlight drifted in and out of the night clouds over us. I listened to insects singing as I fell asleep. Billy shook me awake, and I wondered why.

"We are going up the street to see the tent."

I sat up, then followed Billy and Jack across the porch, out to the sidewalk, across the street, up the next block. We were barefoot. The cement felt warm, and I could feel twigs and dirt in the cracks. Then I felt something brush against me. Remembering the bear, I felt short of breath with fright. Jack whispered in my ear, "There's a big dog beside you."

Relieved, I put out my hand and felt his fur. When we came to the house on the corner, I told Billy that the tent was in its back yard

"Stay here," he said.

He disappeared. The dog sat down. I sat beside him. Jack hid behind a tree. After Billy returned, we walked slowly home, enjoying the night adventure.

I liked summers at our white house on Cheyenne. I could hear the birds singing, the piano playing, the croquet balls clicking, and Grandmother's records playing upstairs. And I smelled roses and fresh-cut grass.

After dinner, if Jack and Billy were there we played hide-and-go-seek. One of us yelled "Alley alley oops, all's out in free!" The game was intense—a wild run to find a hiding place under the cedars or lilac bush or behind the kitchen steps, and then standing still with your heart pounding as you saw the other side searching for you. Then run. Or no, don't run, not yet. Now run fast and go behind the grape arbor.

The whistle meant bedtime. Aw, do we have to go? But we walked quietly into the house. After we were in bed, they came to see us, carrying their iced tea glasses and telling us funny things that happened during the day. Some very warm nights we were allowed to sleep on pallets in the side yard.

Neighborhood Birthday Party 1923 with Jack, Jane, Lydia
and Billy on the far right

One afternoon Mother told us she had invited our new neighbor for tea.
The woman had a son about our age. She said they were renting the house
next door to the Yanceys. Everyone else owned their houses. When you
spoke of a person who rented, you said, "They rent."

We went upstairs to change our clothes. Lena fussed over my hair and
put a bow in it. Billy came in and told us he was going to take charge of
the meeting. Jack said he thought it would be nice to have a new friend.
We went down to the living room and were introduced to Robert and his
mother. Jack and I said hello, but Billy did not speak. We were told to go
out on the porch. Lena brought us a tray with cookies and our homemade
ginger ale. As she turned to leave, she rolled her eyes at us, and we knew
that meant, "Mind your manners!"

I sat in the swing and Jack sat on the footstool. Billy was in the large
rocking chair with his legs crossed. He kept swinging one foot and staring
at Robert.

Finally, Billy asked, "Robert, can you skate on one leg crossover?"

"No," Robert answered, taking another cookie.

"Can you shinny down a drain pipe?"

"No." Robert finished his second cookie and began to drink his ginger ale.

"Would you eat worms?"

Robert finished his ginger ale, put the glass on the tray, turned to Billy, and said, "Never." Then he began to laugh and made a loud gas noise in his pants.

Billy acted horrified and said, "How could you do a thing like that in front of us! How could you be so rude!"

Robert left the porch and ran home.

Pauline with Chinese Screen at Kenwood

On quiet afternoons after school, I liked to walk around our house, room after room, enjoying the things I loved about each one. They were always just the same—clean and neat, with each chair or vase or teapot in the same place. My favorite was our breakfast room with its ornate Chinese cabinet, tall wide Chinese screen covered with ivory birds and flowers, and the black silk drapes with tiny gold embroidered figures. One Friday, Mother interrupted my rounds by calling me into the living room. She introduced me to Mrs. Pepper and explained she had brought Billy and Jack while their parents vacationed.

I saw a large woman sitting in the wingback chair by the bookcases. Her gray hair was marcelled, and she wore wire spectacles. Her white linen and lace blouse had an embroidered collar. A gold chain with an attached locket hung around her neck. Noticing that I liked the locket, she told me she carried a picture of Pep in it. Mother said they had just arrived, and Mrs. Pepper had not changed her traveling suit. They went upstairs so Mother could make her comfortable in the front bedroom. I listened to them talk as they went, and I wished that I had a friend too.

Mrs. Pepper liked to spend time in the kitchen. She made delicious brownies for us. One afternoon when I came home, the kitchen table was covered with round fruit cakes. I could smell baked fruit and nuts and the brandy she and Mother had poured on the wonderful cakes. Later they sealed them in tins and put them in the Chinese cabinet. They locked the cabinet door.

"Not until Christmas," Mother said, looking at me.

The next morning I joined Billy and Jack in the side yard. "Have you read what she wrote in our bathroom?" Billy said. We waited for him to tell us. He said, "Follow me," so we went into the kitchen and up two steps to the little bathroom under the stairs.

We stood looking at the mirror over the sink, moving our mouths in silence as we read, "Don't leave the brown in the toilet." We looked at each other in disbelief, as if to say, Who would do a thing like that?

After we returned to the yard, Billy said, "I don't like her. She has a mole on her face."

Jack said, "How dare you say that about our grandmother! She is nice, and she bakes us brownies."

Billie began waving his hands in the air and singing in a loud voice, "Don't leave the brown in the toilet."

Jack never argued with Billy. He just walked away and went across the street toward Robert's house. I went to the front porch and sat on the swing because Perry skated down the hill to our house every Saturday morning.

The first time I heard Perry's skates, I had jumped out from behind bushes at the end of the sidewalk. He fell into the embankment.

47

"Why did you do that?" he asked.

"Because I wanted to see your skates and find out where you are from."

He said he lived in the house up at the end of the next block. I realized that he lived near the boy who tied me in a tent. Then Perry taught me to skate.

Now every Saturday he rolled down, untied his skates, and sat in our swing so all of us could talk. Mother enjoyed his visits. She said he would be a dark handsome Scotsman with good manners. He was not allowed to attend school but had a tutor every day.

Jack returned from Robert's house just as Julia, in her gentle way, appeared from the south side yard. She had long straight brown hair, very tan skin, and gray eyes. She sat by Perry on the swing. Mother opened the side door and brought us homemade root beer. Billy followed and sat in the other wicker chair, across from Perry. Billy stared at Julia.

Perry took a glass of root beer and handed it to Julia. When Mother gave him another, he said, "I heard that the older boys were going to build a clubhouse somewhere down in the woods by the river."

"Near the path by the river or up near their back yards?" Jack asked.

Perry looked at me and asked, "Do you know where that is?"

"Yes. Once I had to find my way home from there."

Everyone was silent, thinking about the clubhouse and what it meant.

"I would not be allowed to join, even if they asked me," Perry said. "My mother would not let me."

Jack changed the subject: "I heard something down at Robert's house."

We waited. Finally Mother said, "Jack, what did you hear?"

"Well, this is a secret. We cannot tell it to anyone. Louise is dead." No one said anything. Jack repeated, "Louise is dead."

"Now, Jack," Mother said. "Is this really true?"

"Yes."

Louise had lived in a large stucco house next to the Yeagers across Cheyenne. They were the last two houses on that side of the street, down near the river. She had one older red-haired brother. He was always with the Yeagers' two sons. I had not met Louise but I knew she was about three years older than me. They all seemed so grown up. I acted as if I did not know them.

Robert's mother had told Jack that the death was kept secret because Louise had spinal meningitis. They did not want the city authorities to know. Robert's mother said that Aunt Louella, next door, had claimed it was because the child did not have good German food to eat.

The following Saturday we waited for Perry to skate down to our house. Then Mother told us that Perry would not be able to visit and probably would never skate again. He had been sick with a fever, and when he tried to get out of bed, he fell.

We were very sad. Then we heard that the girl across the street could not use one of her legs after a fever. We were told to stay at home and not jump out of trees, because that's what Louise used to do. Now Billy sat on the swing where Perry had always been, by Julia.

Edwina and Pep sometimes spent months at a lake house in Michigan's North Woods. One day they sent us a long dark half-size trunk. Roy found deer hides in it and said it did not belong in a house, so he put it at the bottom of the basement stairs. Later, Jack and I returned from one of our excursions with some small snakes in a bucket. We put the bucket behind the daybed in the breakfast room. When Billy came in, we proudly showed him our snakes.

Billy began running all over the house yelling, "Jane and Jack have snakes in the house!"

We knew we were in trouble. Jack grabbed the bucket, and we ran to the basement. When we saw the trunk, I lifted the lid and he poured the snakes in. We ran back up, returned the bucket to the place behind the daybed, and sat trying to look innocent. Mother, Lena, Roy, and Billy soon arrived to see the snakes.

Billy pointed and said, "They are in the bucket."

Jack carefully lifted the bucket. Roy took it in case the snakes were dangerous.

"No snakes," he said.

Billy insisted, "I saw snakes!"

Jack and I stared blankly at him and asked, "What snakes?"

When Edwina came for the boys, she told Lena to take the hides out and air them in the yard.

Lena's scream echoed through the house. She ran up the stairs calling, "Miz Sheppard! Miz Sheppard! They's a snake in the trunk!"

Roy went down and found no snake in the trunk. He searched the basement. When he moved the woodpile, he saw a large gray snake.

Jack and I went outside to play ball and giggle.

Julia lived in the large white house next door, the last house on our block. She came to see Billy and Jack and me almost every day, and we liked her. This day we were sitting under the large mulberry tree talking about the Fourth of July picnic when she came. As she sat, tears ran down her cheeks. She told us her little sister had died. She had told us about a baby sister the stork brought them last month, but we had not seen the baby. We were all very quiet.

I thought of the field south of her house where we set off firecrackers. It went down to the river, the beautiful river. I thought of another river, another time. Sandy banks and large trees. Then I realized I had not been listening. I heard Billy say, "What is it like?"

So I said, "What is what like?" Billy said, "To be dead."

Julia stood up to go home. I took her hand and walked with her.

When I returned, Jack said, "Listen, they cannot have the neighborhood Fourth of July picnic over there this year."

I nodded. Then I wondered what the sister looked like, and what it was to be dead.

We heard Lena call us to come in for half-and-half. When we were seated, she asked, "Do you chillun know what happened next door?"

We all answered, "Julia told us."

Lena said, "Lawsey, don't you go playin' round there tomorrow."

We ate our cream and graham crackers quietly. When Lena went into the pantry, Billy said he wanted to see the baby sister.

"So do I," I said.

Jack shook his head "No."

We slid off our chairs and went to the stair landing to plan the visit. Jack said he would be the scout. He would find a long stick, tie a white cloth to it, and wave it when the coast was clear. He would stay behind the bush in front of our house.

The next morning Jack saw Julia in her front yard. She said her sister was in a white box on the back sunporch. He reported to us and went looking for a stick. About nine o'clock he crawled into the big white flowering bushes near the front of their house. Billy and I waited in the grape arbor.

When we saw the stick waving, we crept along the sidewalk behind their porch. I opened the door. We tiptoed over to the beautiful white satin box on the table. We stood on our toes so we could see inside. There was a tiny person lying asleep on white satin and lace.

"Touch her and she will wake up," Billy said.

I put my hand inside the box and touched her face. Her skin was cold like the stones I picked up at the river. I felt strange all over. I looked at Billy, and he looked at me.

We heard a voice in the room next to the porch. We ran out and across the drive to the field and crouched in its deep weeds. A long black car entered the driveway and stopped beside the porch. The driver went to the back of the car and opened a door. Then he went inside the porch. Soon he returned with the box and put it in the car. He backed out and drove away.

We stood up and walked around their servants' quarters to our house. Jack was waiting.

"Did you see her?"

"Yes." That's all we said. We never spoke of being dead again.

Several days later, we heard that the Fourth of July picnic would be up at Joan's house, next to Pete's. We had some reservations about going there. She was younger than us. When she had come down to watch us swim in our pool, she always had a doll. She was short and fat with very blonde hair she never combed.

Billy did not like her. Once when he yelled, "Go home, dummy," she cried and wet her pants. Then he yelled, "Go home, wet pants."

Jack told me, "Do something."

So I got out of the pool, put on my pinafore, and walked home with her. When we reached her house, she begged me to come in and see all her dolls. We were taught not to go into any house without our parents' permission. I followed her in.

It seemed empty. Yellow net curtains hung in the living room and dining room. The living room had one couch, two chairs, and a small rug. We went to a staircase on the left side of the room. It did not have a carpet. At the top of the stairs I followed Joan but looked into the bedroom on the right. It too had yellow curtains. A man sat on the side of the bed. A big fat woman sat at a dressing table. She did not have any clothes on. She looked in a mirror as she put on a long strand of beads that draped over her fat stomach.

We went into Joan's room with all the dolls. She started explaining their names. I said, "Joan, who was the woman in that room down the hall?"

"Oh, that was Mama and Uncle Boo."

I thought, as Jean rambled on, Something is wrong here. We don't sit around with our clothes off. I wanted to go home. Then a tall girl entered the room wearing a black dress, silk stockings, and black high heels. She was Joan's older sister.

"Come on," she said. "Let's drive down to the Quaker Drug on Eighteenth and have a cherry Coke."

She had a small bouquet of gardenias tied on her dashboard. The seats were black leather, and the real wood was highly polished. It was so nice. When we went into the drugstore, the soda jerk knew Joan's sister. He fixed our drinks and talked to her a long time before she drove me home.

The Fourth of July finally arrived. We were given a few fireworks to play with in the morning. We put spit devils on the sidewalk and kicked them with our heels until they popped. We lit tiny pills that would crawl. The rest of the day was long, as we were too excited to sleep during nap time. Finally we were told to get ready.

Lena was curling my hair around her fingers and brushing it into long curls when Mother came into the bathroom. She said, "I saw you come home in that Rolls Royce the other afternoon." I told her about Joan's sister.

Mother asked, "What was her mother like?" I thought about the yellow curtains and Mama and Uncle Boo. I knew we wouldn't go if I told her. I said it was a nice house full of yellow curtains, and Joan had a lot of dolls.

When we were all ready, Mother called us into the living room for instructions about going to a new place for the celebration. "We will leave soon," she said. Oh, we waited. Finally, the sun set. After that came the last glow we called the golden hour, when the light makes lovely colors everywhere.

Roy came into the hall carrying two oblong woven baskets of food. Mother came down the stairs dressed in white linen. She began the procession, then the three of us. Roy followed, walking very straight. As we went up Cheyenne, other neighbors joined us. Roy always bowed to them, and when he saw their maids he would smile and say, "How-dee do."

The block from Eighteenth to Nineteenth was closed. Tables and chairs lined the street. In front of Joan's house sat her "Mama" wearing a large flowered dress that went down to her ankles. And the beads. My mother pressed her lips together and her dark eyes went cold. That moment passed as we joined the laughter.

We had everything we had ever dreamed of to celebrate with. There were bushel baskets of fireworks, with Roman candles and skyrockets. The party lasted long after our bedtime. We walked home exhausted. Billy kept asking, "Did you see this? Did you see that?" Jack and I stumbled along, not able to answer.

Home at last. As we climbed the stairs, Grandmother stood by the banister. She said, "Cox's army marching through Georgia."

The Peters invited all the neighborhood children to a party at their pool before closing it for the winter. Lena told me to put on my bathing suit with a dress over it. I really did not want to go, but Billy had told everyone he would ride his bicycle off the diving board. I had to see that.

I walked up Cheyenne with Jack while Billy rode his bicycle in and out around the tall elm trees. We looked over at Perry's house, thinking about him. He was on his front porch, and we could see him waving at us. Jack said, "Let's go see him."

Billy went on, but Jack and I walked up the steps and sat beside Perry on the swing. His paralyzed legs were covered with a plaid car blanket. He wanted to know everything we had been doing. Then he told us that the boys' clubhouse had been built behind two houses across Cheyenne from our house. He told us to go see it and tell him all about it and who was in the club. We promised.

Then a tall woman with a knot of gray hair appeared at the door. When she saw us, she stepped out and told us to leave. Perry asked if we could stay. She looked at me and said she would have him carried into the house if we did not leave. I wanted to stay but could see that she did not like us. We left and continued walking toward the party. Jack said that when we found out about the clubhouse we could tell Perry from the side of his porch where she could not see us.

By then we had climbed up the small embankment toward the great Council Oak Tree. We saw Billy riding his bicycle toward us. But he was across the street, going home. Since we did not want to go swimming anyway, we followed Billy back home.

Mother saw us from the porch and asked Jack and me what happened. We did not know, so she called Billy. He finally came. "What did you do?" she asked.

He told us he had the bicycle on the diving board and was just getting ready to climb on and roll into the pool when a woman screamed at him, "Get down from there, you terrible boy! Get off our property!"

Mother said he should have apologized and that he should not try that again, anywhere. She told him he would understand when he grew older that certain things are not acceptable.

We did not know the rules of grown-ups because we lived in our own world where time circled around us. We did not know that the long summer days of play would never return.

Billy asked us what we talked about with Perry. We told him about the clubhouse, so he planned a scouting trip. Several days later, he said we had to have a meeting down at the cave. The next morning when Jack and I crawled in, Billy was already there. He had candles burning in the small alcoves and had drawn a map of the clubhouse location.

He said, "I have found the place. I'm mad because they did not invite me to become a member." Jack and I remained silent. Billy continued, "I have a plan that will surprise them, and we can blame it on the boy who lives up at the corner—the one who tied Jane in a tent."

I said that he never came out of his house. And that episode was over. But before I could finish, Billy insisted, "You just listen to me. We are going to do this. I have it all planned."

The plan was that we would pull sour grass, put it in a bucket, and let it get smelly. Then I would climb up on his shoulders and into the tree behind the clubhouse. Jack would hand Billy the bucket, and he would lift it up to me to pour into the stovepipe.

Jack asked, "Will they have a fire in the stove?"

Billy said, "Of course they will have a fire with a coffee pot on it, like grownups."

I told him I was going to tell Lena and Roy about it because I did not want to get into trouble. We crawled out of our cave and went to the basement to talk to Lena. She said she would make me a grass blanket to hide under, and Roy would watch things.

On the evening of a club meeting, Billy boosted me up to the first branch of the overhanging tree. Then he took the bucket from Jack and passed it to me. Gradually switching hands, I climbed farther up. Billy and Jack ran across Cheyenne and behind our house to the cave. I listened to the boys inside the clubhouse talking. Then I poured the mixture into the stovepipe. As white smoke came out of the pipe, boys ran through the door yelling. I climbed down a few branches then jumped out of the tree and crawled under the grass blanket. I heard the boys running toward the woods along the river, the way I was supposed to escape.

So I ran to the back of the yard where Johnny lived. He was an older boy who was always nice to all of us. I thought he looked like the picture of a prince in my storybook. I heard his back screen door squeak and saw him come out. I quickly climbed up the nearest tree and held very still. I knew he was going to see what had happened at the clubhouse. As he walked under the tree, the branch I was sitting on broke, and I fell behind him. I was never so embarrassed in my life.

He said, "Jane! Why are you here? Are you hurt?"

I stood up and tried to be calm. I told him I had been walking in the woods when I heard those boys yelling, so I ran up there to hide from them.

"Come with me," he said. "We will go see what happened."

Nicky came walking toward us. He had been in the clubhouse and asked, "Did you see anyone?"

I crossed my fingers behind my back and said, "Yes. I saw Pete, that boy who lives up at the corner, running home."

I had told a bad fib. But after I thought about that day in the tent, it was not such a bad fib. Nicky and Johnny left, and I walked across Cheyenne, past our house, past the quarters, down the hill to the cave. I told Billy I would never do anything like that again, and he could keep all his crazy plans to himself.

Jack said, "Bud, what good did it do? You did not change things." But Billy felt triumphant.

After dark, Roy went over and brought back the grass blanket.

When Pawnee and Mike next visited, their Sonny had become deaf from an infection. He was a little older than Jack, so he became part of our group, though he could not hear us or talk to us. He went to a school for deaf children where he learned to talk with his hands. I learned his sign language later, but now we all just communicated with gestures. He liked to draw. One rainy day when all four of us were in the breakfast room drawing or reading, Billy said we should find something to do. Then he announced, "Let's go upstairs and explore the attic."

We did not know where the grown-ups were, so we tiptoed through the house and up the steep attic stairs. The family always left keys in locks, so the attic was easy to open. Once inside, we sat and looked around the long room where we were sometimes allowed to play. The ceiling was shaped like our peaked roof. Three small windows let in light. The attic bookcases were only two shelves high because of the slanting walls. That left stacks of Father's law books bound in leather with gold lettering, art books by Christie and Flagg, the Little Colonel series, and many others on the wide planked floors.

We found a very old carved wooden toy circus set. All its performers had movable arms and legs and were pegged together on wooden horses and elephants. Then we began opening boxes and the old family trunks. We were in wonderland.

The tall box with folding sides held a three-tiered cake with a bride and groom standing on top. Faded paper ivy and tiny silver bells twined around columns holding the tiers. White roses around the bottom looked good to eat, so I broke off a piece. It was very hard sugar. We each ate a rose.

On a lace pillow in one trunk I found Fanchion, the doll Grandmother told me that her mother always kept on her bed. I was so excited that I closed the trunk. Then I opened it, carefully lifted her, and held her in my arms. She had large blue eyes and curly blond hair. She wore a rose taffeta dress with ruffles, a petticoat, and pantaloons. Her china hands and feet were attached to a cloth body filled with sawdust. When I put her back, I noticed a strange object under the lace pillow. I pulled it out and realized it was a hoop skirt made of netting between covered metal rings.

Billy's trunk had a flat black hat that he said was beaver, like Lincoln wore. He popped it up, put it on his head, and found a long black coat. Jack found a man's black and gray striped coat with tails. Sonny put a derby hat on his head, held a cane, and began imitating Charlie Chaplin. We all laughed.

Billy said, "Let's build a stage and play act."

We saw a mattress for our stage. Jack stacked books in front of it for seats. The play began. Billy looked very important in his tall hat and long coat proclaiming, "Friends, Romans, and countrymen!" Then he told the story of Romulus and Remus. We clapped, and he bowed.

Next, Jack began, "The rain is raining all around . . ." and recited the Stevenson poem. We clapped, and he bowed.

I tied the hoop skirt around my neck and wore a flowered hat. I said I was a singer from New York, then sang a song Grandmother had taught me, "See the boat go round the bend. . . ."

While I waved goodbye to the imaginary boat, my leg caught in the hoopskirt and I fell off the mattress. I landed beside a window and noticed something green between the wooden floor planks. When Jack came to help me up, I moved so we could all see the green object. We were wondering how we could move the board when we heard the attic door open. We quickly moved away from the hidden treasure.

Lena said, "Lawsey, lawsey. Jes look at you young-uns!" We stood very still. "Git that finery off, put it back, and come down and clean up for dinner." We dutifully obeyed.

We always went to the side yard after dinner, but it was still raining. Billy wound up the Victrola, and we sat around the living room. Jack said we had to share our secret with someone so we would know what was under the boards. Billy thought it might be a secret way to the roof.

The next day, we found Roy sitting on the basement steps carving a wooden chain. We told him what we had seen.

"Wellum," he said. "I will see about it."

Later he told us that when men laid the floor they had left broken glass under it. We listened, but we thought maybe Billy was right. It was a secret way to the roof.

Years later, I made a studio of the attic. All the old things had been moved, leaving the floor clear. I pried up a board and found bottles of fine champagne Father and Roy had hidden. I sat the bottles on a table by the window for a while, then returned them. It was now my secret.

Travels with Mother

I heard that Pawnee and Wells had met in St. Louis then gone to the horse races in Kentucky. They lost all their money betting, so they went to a pawn shop and pawned their diamonds. Then they called Father. He had to buy it all back and then some.

Several days later, a telegram came from St. Louis to say Wells had married that man who smoked a pipe. The scene was terrible. Mother ran back and forth from the living room to the dining room screaming and wailing, waving the telegram over her head. I sat on the stairs by my dolls watching her. Grandmother came out of her room upstairs, went to the banister, and banged her crutch on it. She called, "Lit!" in a loud voice.

Mother stopped and went into the living room. I went upstairs to sit with Grandmother. She said, "I am glad. She will not be in this house any more. No formal wedding! What a disgrace."

Not long after that, I was on a train again. This time Mother and I were going to see the newlyweds in Lebanon, Illinois. We did not talk. I just listened to train sounds. Sometimes our train stopped and another train rushed by, whistles echoing as it rolled down the track. We arrived at the St. Louis station, an enormous Gothic place where trains from all over the country met. It had very high ceilings and many oak benches. People stood around or sat with grips, boxes, and bags. Children with no expressions on their faces stood by their parents. No one talked. We waited too.

Jane and Lydia on Earlier Trip

A woman had made a bed for her child on part of our bench. When it began to cry, she picked it up and held it over her shoulder. It had pink eyes and white hair. I looked at Mother, but she turned away. Later she said I had seen an albino. She said they never change.

Then Wells and Tom came. He picked up our grips and led us to their car. We drove across the Mississippi River, through East St. Louis, on to Lebanon. He said most people there spoke German. He showed us an estate and said he was related to the family that owned it, as well as a large flour mill. We drove down the main street and turned in at a garage in the middle of town. Other cars and a fire truck were parked inside. He led us up wooden stairs to their apartment.

After dinner, Wells told us they had a pet monkey that in daytime they used to tie to the garage front door. When the large German women carried their market baskets by, the monkey would jump out, grab something out of their baskets, and run up to the door top. Now the monkey was kept in back by the water well. Tom told us to come to the basement, where he put the monkey at night. We followed him carefully as there were auto parts everywhere. In the corner, a cat slept on a mattress.

"Watch what the monkey does," he said, as he turned it loose. The monkey grabbed the cat and climbed on its back. The cat cried and tried to get away. I thought this was terrible, but they were laughing.

The next morning I needed something to do. Mother said I could go out but to be back by three in the afternoon. In the back yard, I found a well with a long iron handle. A chain came up with small oblong buckets. Water spilled from the buckets as I pumped the handle. Dark green ivy covered a red brick wall, and a tree leaned against the ivy. Under it was an old wooden table.

I saw the monkey climb down from the tree to the table. I thought he would be nice to play with, like my cat, Tinkerbell. I said, "Hello, little monkey." He grabbed my arm and leaned over to bite me. I put my hand on his head, leaned over, and bit his ear. He ran up the tree chattering and squeaking.

I hung on a honeysuckle vine to climb over the fence then jumped down to a sidewalk. I walked along the street and around town. I did that all week. Once I took the purse Pawnee had given me and I went to the drugstore. I wanted a cherry Coke, but the man said he was going to fix me something new. It was a green river—just like a limeade only much greener.

Saturday they said we were going to the park. Mother and Wells cooked food for our baskets. When we arrived, everyone else also had baskets of sausages, pork ribs, roasts, sauerkraut, melons, sweet rolls, streusel, and cakes. I heard people speaking German. The band played German music that all sounded the same, "Oom pah pah, oom pah pah." All the food was put on one long table, and everyone took helpings. I stayed at our table, and Mother brought me a plate. She told me to eat some hot potato salad. Then I was thirsty, so I picked up a cup of cold beer near my plate and drank all of it.

Soon I began to feel very strange. I thought I had better sit on the ground, but instead I fell. "Hey," Tom said, "Look at her. Ha ha!"

Mother picked me up and took me to the park bathroom. She told me to hang my head over and put a finger down my throat. Afterward she made me feel better with her cold wet handkerchief on my face. Then we walked back through the crowd to our table. I did not eat. I wanted to go home. I hated being there.

I was told to go to the bandstand and stay because they were going to walk around and visit. From the top step, I could see other children running and playing. Most people sang and clapped their hands. Women in bright dresses of purple, red, blue, and yellow were putting more food on plates. I noticed that the men wore shirts without ties. I watched patterns of shade and sunlight across the whole scene while I waited for that long afternoon to end.

Finally, we were going back to Tulsa. Again, I was in the back seat with all the grips. We were driving behind a large truck full of cantaloupes when the back gate of the truck broke and cantaloupes rolled out. Some split, splashing fleshy light orange centers on the highway. Some rolled into roadside grass. They just kept falling. Tom quickly stopped, got out of the car, and ran around picking up cantaloupes. He opened the back door and threw them all over the back seat. I pulled my legs up as they hit me. I could see another driver helping put cantaloupes back in the truck, but our car backed up and continued to the train station.

"All aboard," the conductor said. I closed my eyes and listened to the sound of wheels on rails. At last I was going home. Looking back, I wondered why I was taken to Lebanon. I decided Mother wanted to see Wells and thought I should not be at home without supervision while Father was in Muskogee.

When we returned to our home, I wanted to see if everything was the same. Lena was in the kitchen. She said Napoleon had gone to the river, caught some large catfish, and put them in the swimming pool. Roy had built a trap to catch a possum. Gertrude had gone visiting but left me a note. Her scrawl read, "Everybody are gone, and I is blues." Lena added that Grandmother had been ailing.

Grandmother always had bad pains in her legs. She said they began when she was a girl because at that time of the month she jumped into a creek to cool off. Sometimes Roy took her a glass of bourbon for relief—another secret.

When I went to her room, she told me Roy had taken her to a doctor who said he could give her monkey glands for her legs and she would get better. Grandmother said, "I would not have them. I might climb the bedpost." I noticed her fancy popcorn spread was not on the bed, so I sat beside her. She took my hand and told me how glad she was to have me home.

I do not remember much about the next few weeks. I had a bad fever, then puffy bumps and sores all over my body. I could see Grandmother's face beside my bed, the bun of her gray hair, and her brown eyes as she put damp leaves on my face. Sometimes I heard her tell me to drink water. Sometimes I wondered why I was in bed. Sometimes I thought I had walked into an old deserted house, and I kept trying to find the way out.

Finally everything began to be real again. I could sit up and sip the onion broth she held in front of me. The sick feeling left, but I was very weak. Days later, Grandmother burned the fumigation candle to kill all the germs in the room. Now I could go into other parts of the house. People had to be very careful about any sickness. If the city found out, the sick person would be taken someplace and kept until they recovered.

Lena said since I was over the pox and Roy had to go uptown shopping, I could ride with him. The town began at First Street, and the business district was seven or eight blocks. The rest of Main Street and the streetcar rail came south only to Eighteenth Street.

First Roy drove uptown to a filling station east of Main. It was on a corner and had a large blue dome roof. Then he said he had to go get some food for himself in Greenwood, the burned-out town north of our town that was just for them. He parked at a low stone building. He carried me in. On the wall behind the bar there was a picture of Haile Selassie. He was their king. Roy bought some smoky smelling meat wrapped in brown paper. He said they made it there, and it was barbeque.

I asked if he could drive to the drugstore on Eighteenth and get a cherry Coke for me. I told him the soda jerk's name was Farrel. After he parked and went in, I decided to go inside too. But I stopped because I saw large machines down the hill in the valley—in what had been the woods where I kept my Chinese box. I knew it was gone forever. The machines were clearing a wide space, and men were building a tall half-round structure.

Beautiful old trees lay on the ground. Dirt was piled everywhere. Destruction beyond belief.

I began to cry. Roy came back with the drink and asked why I was crying. I could only point to the disaster down the hill. He said he would drive us down the school road, Boulder, so I could see the rest of it. There I looked at the hill I used to climb down to enter the north end of the woods.

As I sobbed, I told Roy all about my forest. He said he would clear another area behind our house so I could have a place to go. And he would add a new cave against the hill. I did not tell him that one time when I was looking for butterflies I saw a man down there. He was carrying a brown burlap bag on his back, and he had a long black beard and a cap. Then I had run very fast to the house, up the stairs, and into my closet. I sat in the dark listening to my heart beat. I could go to that woods only when Billy and Jack were with me.

Roy added that the barn was going to be taken out. A big sewer would follow that creek down to the river. My paradise was gone forever.

After we had lived in Tulsa for several years, Mother said she and I were going east for the summer. Usually we went with Father, but he could not leave his business. So I had Mother all to myself. First we went to New York City. Mother shopped for dresses while I walked around behind her. She and my sisters always bought their clothes in New York at Wanamaker's and Saks.

After days of shopping, we went up the Hudson River to see Mike Fanning's sister, Kate. She was married to an Italian count named Antonio Sarow. They lived near the river in a place I thought was wonderful. While Mother and Kate talked about the family, I sat by the window and watched boats. We stayed for a dinner served on a red checkered tablecloth. Kate's white maid prepared bowls of grated cheese, crumbled bacon, ground meat, and tomato sauce. She piled hot spaghetti high on our plates. We passed the bowls around and each of us selected what we wanted on our spaghetti. We took breadsticks from an upright holder that resembled a rooster. It was all difficult to eat but delicious.

The next day we took a train to Columbus, Ohio to visit Pawnee and Mike and Sonny. I was so excited to see them waiting for us on the platform. After many hugs we drove to their house and settled in for a two-week vacation.

Sonny and I still shared his world silently. I nodded my head when I understood him. He showed me how to walk on the back fence and how to find mealy bugs. He had a trick of putting crossed straight pins on the streetcar track. When the car passed, the smashed pins looked like scissors.

Mike liked sports. He took us to a boxing match where we sat with Jack Dempsey and his wife. Mike liked Jack, and we thought him very polite. And Mike taught us to sing "Oh, oh, Ohio" because Ohio State University was there. His alma mater was Notre Dame. He talked about Knute Rockne, its famous football coach.

Mike Fanning as "Alf"

Mike wrote a column called "Alf" for a large newspaper. One morning he took me with him. I saw the presses roll, the typesetters, and the city desk where the editor sat among the other men who wrote news stories. It was very busy with phones ringing, typewriters clicking, and men moving about.

Mike took me to the art department, a long room with large windows on one side. Part of the room had a rug and small table. The rest was a clutter of easels and tables covered with paints and brushes. The back wall had cartoons and old headlines pinned on it. Mike introduced me to Harry Westerman, the artist. He was middle-aged, thin, with gray eyes and light brown hair. Mike said I could sit there for about an hour. Harry showed me his work. I was speechless, but I wanted so much to tell him how wonderful I thought it was, and how I wanted to be an artist. I just nodded and waited for Mike.

When he came, Harry said, "Could you bring her back tomorrow? I want to do a painting of her for the art show."

I posed wearing a red linen sleeveless dress and tan sandals, with one arm resting on the side of a dark green chair. I watched people in a courtyard below as they wandered on the brick walks or sat on wooden benches reading newspapers and feeding pigeons. Pigeons were everywhere. Sometimes a dog ran after them, and they flew to building tops, then back.

While I was sitting for Harry, my mother and sister went to matinees. Pawnee said she was just wild about Rudolph Valentino. He was a screen idol. She had a record of him singing a song from the movie *The Sheik*. The song said something about creeping into your tent at night. I did not know why anyone would want that man to creep into their tent.

We ate lunch in a beautiful restaurant near the newspaper. Wrought iron rails lined the steps leading down to antique glass doors. They opened on a large room that had tables covered with white cloths and crystal glasses. One side of the room was lined with cases holding live tropical fish. Sonny was enchanted.

After lunch, Mike took us to the center of town, where we saw Houdini hang by a rope and untie himself. I did not like it. "Why does he want to do that?" I asked Mike.

He explained that Houdini was a showman and magician and that was how he made his living. I remembered the man who rode a bicycle around the roof edge of the Severs in Muskogee.

One evening, we went to the theater. We were ushered to our seats by girls wearing hoop skirts with tiny lights pinned on them. The girls looked like walking Christmas trees. I kept watching them instead of the show.

The following Sunday we went to an amusement park. It had square white wooden posts on each side of the entrance, with an archway overhead holding the name "Dreamland." Entering, we all became the same age. Wonderful old elm trees shaded paths that led to rides and concessions. There were tables and benches by a small lake for picnics, or you could put a quilt on the grass. We sat on benches watching people ride the merry-go-round. I thought the horses were beautiful.

"Could we buy a horse like that?" I asked.

Mike said, "They are carved in Europe and made only for parks."

"Where do they go when they get old?"

"Men fix them and put them back." I still wished for one.

Mother said the merry-go-round music made her think of the stern-wheeler on the Ohio River. Pawnee remembered going over to Ohio on it.

I said, "It had a large red wheel."

Everyone looked at me. Mother asked, "How did you know?"

"You put me down and I stood on the deck and watched it churn the water. I was frightened by the sound and movement and could not cry out." I remembered a fear that made me only see and hear.

Pawnee mentioned the men going from Huntington up the Ohio to Catlettsburg to buy champagne for her wedding at Kenwood. She still had their wedding pictures on her dresser.

Mother added, "Remember Liza, who worked for us?"

Then Pawnee told me that Liza jumped the gate every morning when she came to work. Kenwood was always with them.

Pauline at Kenwood before Wedding

Pauline's Wedding Party at Kenwood 1917
Seated left Edwina and Pep. Wells to left of Mike.

Mike brought us back to reality as Sonny ran across the grass toward the concessions. Mike bought us root beer.

We rode the Caterpillar, a long row of cars on a track that drove through the park. Sometimes a striped awning rolled over us and we were under the Caterpillar. Then it rolled back and we had daylight again. And we rode the Whip. Its cars had high backs and belts across our laps so when we swung out and back we did not fly into space.

Then Sonny found cars like real cars on a dirt track. He got into one and waved at me to get into another. I was too tall and old for the little cars, but I took the steering wheel and we drove away. Mike motioned that we could go around two times. I stopped after the second, but Sonny drove four laps. Mike paid the man, stepped out on the track, and put his hands up to stop Sonny. I think we could have left Sonny there all afternoon. He was in dreamland.

When we found Mother and Pawnee, they had won a carved plastic Buddha. We rubbed his feet for good luck. Later Mother kept him in the Chinese cabinet at home, and he blended with the authentic art around him.

Mike took me to a place where they were throwing balls at pegs. He said, "Throw real easy, and try the two on the outside." After several lobs, one went down. The man handed me a baby doll wearing a long white dress. Her hands and head were bisque, and her eyes opened and closed.

When Pawnee saw my doll, she said, "Jinsey, I want it." She kept it on her bed for years and pinned her diamonds under its dress.

We were having a grand time, as Grandmother would say. The last ride was the roller coaster. The others waited for us as Mother and I got into one of the wooden cars. Clickety, clickety up the wooden track until we reached the top. Then we went forward with terrible speed. Then down, around curves, and up and over. Mother lost her hat. Mike had to help her out of the car. Mother and I used the expression "like a rollo coaster" from then on. Dreamland was a dear memory.

Jane, Pauline, Sonny and Lydia 1926

The last part of the visit was our trip to West Virginia. First Pawnee took me to a delicatessen for sandwich meats to take on the trip. I had never been to one. It was a small place with a large display of rolled meats. Strange smells and strange foods filled the room. A large man with a black mustache kept asking Pawnee to taste this and that. When he asked me, I shook my head.

Then we were on the road. Sometimes Mike sang and we joined in, and sometimes we just looked at the scenery. We stayed in a place called an inn. It was a hotel made of logs, built against a hill. Mother and I were in a second-floor room on the mountain side. You could walk out on a bridge that crossed to a little park where beautiful ferns grew around rocks. I had to touch them.

We drove another day until we reached an embankment where Mike stopped and pointed to the settlement on the deep green river below us. "That is Harper's Ferry," he said. "Now I will tell you a story about it." As he talked, I realized this was a real story that happened here. I was listening to the history of our country.

I asked, "Why did John Brown do this?"

"He was a fanatic."

What does that mean, I wondered. Then he explained that there were many people who wanted Negro slaves freed. That was hard to understand because I had never thought about what happened to them. We were not told things like that.

When we returned to the highway, Mike quoted the poem about hanging John Brown in the morning. Back at the inn I sat in the park with ferns, feeling the story of Harper's Ferry in my heart. It was very sad.

The next day we drove along narrow roads into tall mountains. When I looked out the window, I was overcome with fear because of deep drop-offs next to the road. Sometimes we climbed a series of turns until we were in clouds, with misty pine trees standing around us. I was not afraid then because the fog reminded me of the river at home.

A small settlement in the valley had a grocery store, a variety store with household goods, and a station for gasoline. When Mike spoke to people there, they did not answer him. While he bought gas, we watched a train pass. Mother said it was the B&O, Baltimore and Ohio.

Another stop was at a large building made of logs. When we entered and smelled the ham turning on a spit, we got hungry. Pawnee said this was a roadhouse, and if you knew the right people you could probably get mountain moonshine. Mike asked if we were on the right road to Logan's cabin. After I ate, I asked to go outside. I went up the mountain, put my arms around a pine tree, then sat on its thick, slippery needles. I looked up into the blue haze.

Back in the car, I asked if people lived up there. Mother said some of them only came out for supplies and never went into the real world. Mike said they spoke a mixture of our English and the old words. What a strange place to live. I missed the flat land at home.

Then we turned off the road to a small path just wide enough for our car. I saw a field and a deserted cabin they called Logan's. I asked if I could get out and walk across the field. Mike asked why, and I said because I had been there before and knew where to walk. Mother didn't think I would remember. I told her the cabin had a dirt floor and a loft with a broken hand-made ladder. They let me out. As I ran across the field, I felt more at home in West Virginia.

Logan's Cabin with Mike, Lydia, Sonny and Jane

Pauline, Sonny, Mike

When Pawnee and Mike left us, I felt so lonely for them. Now we were with Mother's brother Uncle B.B. in his large log cabin. Aunt Anna was polite and always served us ham and eggs and blackberry cobbler for breakfast. Their daughter was in a convent, training to be a nun. Uncle B.B. sat by a big fireplace, even though it was not winter. He had all his pipes on the mantle. In the evening he called his five cats to come to the five bowls of food by the fireplace. I liked him and his cats. One day he told me to go see his chickens. They were in cages with wire bottoms on a bridge he built over the nearby stream. Now he didn't have to clean up after them. After four days, Uncle B.B. drove us to Huntington.

Mother was very tired, so we stayed at a hotel. One day she hired a man to drive us to Kenwood. She got out of the car and stood at the gate. She cried, "Oh, my home! My beautiful home!" I remembered being there too and playing in the yard with Pawnee. I remembered Roy helping me balance on a big log. And I remembered using my walker around the Chinese furniture. We cried together. Then we returned to Oklahoma.

The next year Uncle B.B. and Aunt Anna came to visit us. He was very friendly. Every day after breakfast he told me to get in the car with them, and we would go to the drugstore for chocolate sodas. Aunt Anna always said, "Bilton, tell me which way you are going to turn so I can get situated right." And he always did.

Changes at Home

Edwina and Pep were back in Tulsa again. Grandmother told me it was a disgrace the way she spent all her time down in Muskogee with Father. And she always thought of Father first and Pep second. Grandmother added, "I imagine she is getting rid of John A.'s secretary." Edwina did just that. She had found Mona's brother back in West Virginia and told him where she was. He came to Muskogee and demanded money, saying Father had taken Mona over a state line and disgraced her. Father gave him forty thousand dollars. Grandmother said if Edwina had left everything alone and not been so envious, we would not have become as impoverished.

Late one afternoon, Mother took me with her to the Pepper house. I was glad to see Billy and Jack. When we went out in the yard, Billy said they were moving to Chicago. His father had invented something for the radio, and a company bought it. When we went back in the house, I saw Pep sitting in a black velvet chair with only a black satin robe and black slippers on. He had dark brown hooded eyes and wore a monocle. His hair was combed straight back. I think he had pomade on it, like Valentino. Mother was in their bedroom folding clothes to put in a grip. Billy and Jack and I went into the kitchen. Edwina had made some fudge and told me to try it. I told her it was Lent so I could not eat candy. She insisted it was not candy, so I ate three pieces.

One summer afternoon when Lena had drawn the drapes to keep the heat out, I went into the living room to find a book. I saw a man sitting in the large chair by the fireplace. I thought he would talk to me when I walked to the bookcases, but I sensed he did not want me there. So I skipped out.

"Lena," I said, "Who is that in the living room?"

"Don't you remember your father?"

"He looks so different."

"Don't bother him." Then I found out he was staying with us and sleeping in Mother's bedroom, the long room next to mine, with the fireplace. Sometimes it had been our upstairs living room because the bed was in a small room on its south.

One night I was awakened by Mother's voice telling him to go downstairs because someone was in our house. I quickly got out of bed, went to the hall door, and waited to see what he would do. Then I saw his tall figure in a long white nightshirt holding a candle in one hand and a pistol in the other. As he passed, I stepped into the hall and walked behind him. He went down the carpeted stairs, and I followed. When he turned to the kitchen, I stayed on the last stair. After a muffled sound, the back door slammed. I heard someone running. I slipped up the stairs and hid behind my door. Soon he returned, walking down the hall with the candle, holding the pearl handle of the pistol. I thought he was very brave, and I liked him.

As days went on, he seemed to be far away from us. He never talked to me. Every time I saw him in the living room, he was sitting in the same chair reading law books.

We rested or took naps on hot summer afternoons. I was usually in Grandmother's room in her four-poster mahogany bed. Across from it, she had a matching high dresser with a large clock on top. It had carved Grecian pillars on each side and ornate scrolls on the face. Her clock sounds ticked away our lives. On each side of the clock were tall statues. One was the Virgin Mary in a blue flowing dress. She held a rosary, and her face looked into heaven. The other was Joseph in a light brown robe that went down to the pedestal. His right hand held a lily, and his left hand held a red and gold book. His hair was dark, and he had a beard.

When I was younger and looked at him, I had thought of Simon coming up the stairs after me—that scary man my sisters had told me about in Kenwood. Grandmother had assured me Joseph was not Simon. I had not been too sure.

Grandmother still liked to read me to sleep, often from our set of Dickens. Sometimes we got the box of Edgar Guest's poems out of her trunk. As she read them, she raised her arms and gestured. But late that summer I had to stay alone because she was always in Father's room in case he needed something. I would not take a nap, though. I rocked in her chair, talked to the canary, and hopped up and down the stairs.

One day when I sat with my dolls on the first landing, I saw Father walk out of his room and put his hands on the upper banister. He began speaking about a client. Grandmother stood behind him. When he finished, he turned and walked back into his room. Grandmother blew me a kiss then put her finger to her mouth to keep me quiet.

After dinner, she told Mother, "Lit, he thought he was back in court today and gave a closing speech."

I was back at Holland Hall by now. The headmistress announced that we were going to have outdoor activities, starting with basketball and baseball, then track. She introduced a large broad-shouldered woman called Miss Hume. Miss Hume had very short hair. A silver chain around her neck held a whistle. She wore a white blouse and dark blue pants. I had never seen a woman wear pants. It was confusing.

A basketball court was laid out behind the school. The court had chalked lines and poles at each end with board frames holding rings to throw a ball through. Miss Hume explained the rules to us. She said that girls who did not care for such activity were excused. I could hardly wait for the game to begin.

We played, guarded, jumped, and ran all over the court, with Miss Hume striding along the sidelines, blowing her whistle when we made an error. I was not good at catching a ball, but throwing it through a ring was joy. I had found something wonderful to do. Basketball took all my time after school. I bounced the ball, caught it, leapt, and threw it up toward the ring, trying to loop it in. Often a large old German shepherd dog sat on the banks and watched. He became a friend, and I talked to him about everything. It was so pleasant.

One Sunday, like every other Sunday, I planned to spend the afternoon practicing my new game. Instead, I was told our routine would be different.

We were not going to Mass. The priest was coming to our house. I was not happy with the news because I thought priests in their long black robes were frightening. An air of mystery about religion made me wonder who they really were. During Mass, they walked around in front of the altar speaking Latin. After Mass they sometimes dressed like other men and spoke English.

This Sunday there would be a ceremony at home. I remembered walking down a long aisle in a church dressed in white with a wreath of white flowers on my head. I carried a basket of flowers and scattered petals on the aisle. I was terrified. Ceremonies were designed for us to perform in, and here I was in another one.

The house was darkened against the heat. A candlestick was placed on the marble table with matches beside it. I sat on the stair wearing my Sunday best, waiting for the priest. Soon I heard a knock. I bravely rose, lit the candle, and opened the door. There he stood in a dark robe, holding a prayer book. I could not speak. As he stepped into the hall, I began climbing the stairs. He followed. Candlelight danced as I moved into the darkness. I felt like I could not breathe.

Finally we reached the upstairs hall. I saw Grandmother standing at Father's door. She took the candle, and the priest entered. I went into an adjoining bedroom and fell across the bed. I felt like I had been running a long way. Eventually, curiosity made me get up and go to the door that connected with Father's room. It was slightly open. I saw Father sitting in bed in a dark red satin jacket. Mother stood beside him holding his hand. The priest was performing a marriage ceremony. They had renewed their vows.

Because I had still had to stay inside, I went downstairs, wound the Victrola, and listed to Fritz Kreisler playing his violin while I browsed through books.

Roy helped Father down the stairs so he could have dinner with us. After dinner, Father told Mother to call Harry Bothham and order a new car. She and Grandmother nodded at him. Then I watched them glance at each other as though they shared a secret.

Among our sets of books was one on nature. I studied the book on moths. Then I found *Girl of the Limberlost* about a girl who collected moths. I thought this was a wonderful thing to do, so I asked Roy to build me a cage to keep cocoons in. Then on weekends when he walked along the river to the dairy by the Eleventh Street Bridge, sometimes I went along to look for cocoons.

That summer day when we were returning home with the milk and my day's collection, we saw a car stop at our house. Edwina got out. The driver opened the trunk and carried a grip up the front steps. We ran to the kitchen and found Lena standing behind the door leading to the hall. She turned to us and said, "Hush now."

We heard Mother in the front hall ask, "Edwina, why are you here?"

"I am going to take him with me!"

Mother called upstairs in a loud voice for Grandmother. So it began. For two days you could hear the three women shouting at each other. I kept out of sight. Edwina ran Grandmother out of Father's room. One evening Grandmother motioned me to come into her room and said, "Tell Lena to bring my meals up here until she leaves. I am not going to have anything more to do with these shenanigans."

After several days the house grew quiet. Then that car arrived at our front door again. Roy called it a taxicab. I blended into the cedar tree by the door to watch my father dressed in a suit come out. Roy followed with his grip. Then Edwina came with her eastern suit, hat, and veil. She got into the back seat with Father. The car coasted down the hill toward the river then turned north toward town.

Roy stood on the steps and kept muttering, "Umph, umph." I cried.

That evening only three of us went into the dining room, the room where so much happiness had been created. Roy seated Grandmother at the west end, where the golden sunset circled round her head. He seated Mother at the east end in shadows. Her eyes were red from crying, and she sat very erect. I sat between them with my legs crossed, swinging one back and forth. The golden light ran under my chair and brightened colors on the Oriental rug. We waited in silence for Lena to bring our dinner.

When the swinging door from the pantry opened, she backed into the room as usual, carrying a tray. We unfolded our napkins and smoothed them on our laps. She put the tray on the receiving table and brought a plate to Mother, saying, "Now, Miz Sheppard, I made this just for you." Then she shuffled over to Grandmother and carefully placed a plate before her. As she went back toward the pantry, she turned and shook her head in sadness. I knew I must not, but I wanted to ask why Father left.

After dinner, I excused myself and went to the porch. Its familiar furniture was all white wicker and the floor dark red tile. Green and white striped cloth awnings hung on all sides, topping the tall Ionic posts. As I pushed the swing back and forth, its chains made a creaking sound. I could see other people sitting on porches in the long row of houses across Cheyenne.

Mother and Grandmother came out the side door from the living room. Grandmother sat in the rocker and Mother on the swing beside me. Grandmother always wore white starched blouses, long skirts, and black laced oxfords. She rocked back and forth, and we pushed the swing. Back creak, forth creak. Mother said, "Winter will be late this year."

The night crept around us and sent us to our beds.

Weeks later as I walked across Cheyenne after school, I saw cars around our house. I went to the kitchen, and Lena told me to stay in there. I asked why. Roy stood in front of the sink, looking out the window. He turned and said for Lena to tell me.

She thought a moment. Then she said, "Miz Sheppard and Miz Goings are in the front room with a lot of folks cause Mr. John A. died."

I stood stunned. Then I began to cry.

"Worser than that," Roy added, "that Miz Edwina put him on the train and he was alone." Silence. "I should have been with him." Silence. "I been with him since I was a small boy. How could she do a thing like that!"

Lena kept holding her head down. "It ain't proper the way she did."

The kitchen door opened and we all looked at Grandmother. She said, "Jane, John A. died, and he is coming back on the train alone." Then she added, "To make matters worse, Rain-in-the-Face is coming here with her husband." That was the name she always called Wells.

After Grandmother left, I sat down at the table. Lena put her arm around me and said, "Don't fret yourself none."

For a few days I was not to go to school. Mother and Wells were running around the house searching for something, talking in loud voices. Mother did not know where anything was. They emptied Father's closet and left its contents all over his room. They brought boxes of papers and maps up from the basement and piled them on the kitchen table. Lena had gone to visit Gertrude. Roy went to work for Mr. Travis. Beds were not made, dishes were not washed, and food was not served at the right time.

Grandmother called me to her room. She said, "Close the door and open my trunk." I knew she had been crying. She told me to pull a folder out from under her crazy quilt. When she opened it, I saw a map and some of Father's papers. This was exciting.

She said, "You may sit on my bed because I want to explain something." I nodded. Then she said, "Roy will come tomorrow and carry me down the stairs. Mr. Travis told him to help us. When he leaves, he will take this folder inside his coat. He will send a telegram to John A.'s law partner. This is our secret. You must not speak of it."

I put my hand to my heart and said, "Our secret."

"The next thing I want you to do is look in the back of my closet and find a dark gray cape with black embroidery." I pushed her clothes around and found it. She took it in her arms and said, "John A. liked this cape. I will wear it tomorrow." Her tears fell on it. I wondered what I would wear.

The next morning I went down to the kitchen to find something to eat and a place to eat it. Mother and Wells were already there. I asked them what I should wear to the funeral.

Wells said, "You are not going."

I left my food and went upstairs to Grandmother and told her. She said she could not do anything about it. When I started to leave, she said, "Brush my hair and help me." When Roy came, she looked so nice.

I was crying, heartsick, and felt the strange new pain of anger. When he realized how I felt, Roy said, "Miz Jane, let bygones be bygones."

I stood at the upstairs window and watched them leave. Mother was dressed all in black with a black veil. Grandmother had on her cape. Roy helped her into the long black car. Wells and Tom were last. A man in a black suit closed their door, got in the front seat, and drove away. Then Roy left.

I was alone in an empty house. I went down the stairs, and as I turned toward the kitchen, Grandmother's clock chimed the half hour. I must go to the river, I thought, because if anyone came to the door they would ask why I was not at the funeral. I walked to the cave Roy had built. The roof sagged.

It all seemed so long ago. I realized I had to endure whatever happened. Father had left them to their own destinies. Mine did not matter.

The river was not far, and its sandy bank seemed a safe place to be. Winds scattered leaves around me. Winter was coming. Rains had made the river overflow. Its water created channels through the sand, making the dark earth into brown ribbons. In places where willow trees grew, their low branches trailed designs across the sand. Sometimes when the water was high, I had waded in and held on to a tree so I could watch things float by. Once a shoe seemed like a small boat. Roy had told me there were vagabonds living up north past the bridge. It must have been a shoe from their collection.

This time I walked along the banks only two blocks to where Quicksand Creek had been. The new sewer ended there, covering the valley I had known. Several years ago a large floating log had stopped in the middle of the sandbar. Beyond it lay the deep channel. None of us would go near that deep water, but sometimes we hid behind the log and watched birds.

When I looked over there to see if it was all the same, I saw a figure standing by the log. I was afraid whoever it was would kill one of the birds. Without thinking about the cold and wind, I slid down the bank, walked across the sand, and jumped over some small streams. I finally stood, breathless, in front of an older boy.

He had caught a bird. He said, "Help me hold it."

"You must not hurt it," I said.

"Hold it. It has a broken leg."

I held it. He took out his handkerchief and tore it into strips. He held a small stick against the bird's leg, then wrapped it. I handed him the bird.

"Thanks. I must take it home and care for it. What is your name?" I told him it was Jane.

He started to leave, then said, "My name is Paul."

I walked slowly up the hill and returned home. The house was very quiet. I tiptoed in and up to the stair landing. I gathered the dolls that sat there. Grandmother was asleep, so I went quietly to the kitchen. Lena was back, standing by the stove. The table was still covered with boxes and papers. When she saw me, she said, "Lawsey, Miz Jane. What happened?" We went to the basement.

Life gradually resumed, but some things were different. Mother took me downtown to Miss Jackson's for new dresses. I had to stand in a small room while a woman put them over my head one by one. Then they decided what I should wear. One dress was pale rose and tan with gathers in front and a cloth rose at the waist. I cut the rose off. But I did not have all the things other girls had. The older ones wore silk hose, heels, and lipstick. I did not care. I was still interested in basketball and now track. I ran along the river to prepare for relays.

After Roy left, they had put a front porch on the quarters and called it the little house. Then Wells and her husband moved there. Mother had found him a job in Tulsa through one of her wealthy friends. They ate dinner with Mother, Grandmother, and me every night. They did not talk about anything interesting, only what had happened to them each hour of that day. Listening reminded me of riding over and over on the Caterpillar at Dreamland. Wells was real fat now. They said she was going to have a baby.

I was moved into Father's room, the large bedroom with the brick fireplace. My clothes and shoes were put in his closet on the north side of the room. A small hall connected to the bathroom between that closet and Mother's closet. She kept her clothes in there with her trunk.

Wells, Edwina, Jane, Lydia and Pauline

Every evening after dinner I went to my room. I had been taught to have routines at school and at home. First I shined my shoes and made sure my clothes were ready for the next day. I went into my closet and left the door open so I could see the cabinet that held shoe polish.

As I turned to get it, the door closed.

In the darkness I went toward the door to open it again. Someone stood in front of me. I was pushed against the wall and held there with one hand on my throat. Speechless with fear, I tried to get away, but he pushed his body against me and said, "Now you are going to like this. I am going to help you shine your shoes every night." He tried to put his mouth over mine. I smelled tobacco and felt his mustache. I tried to push him away.

The door opened and I saw my grandmother holding the dark blue pistol from the dining room wine chest. She was pointing it at him. He immediately let me go. She told me in a very quiet voice, "Go get Lit." She motioned with the gun for him to stay in the closet.

When I returned with my mother, my fat sister came along. Amazed, they looked at Grandmother and the gun.

Grandmother said, "I want this Yankee white trash out of the house forever."

My mother looked horrified, and my sister screamed at me, "It's your fault!"

For a long time afterward, I slept with Grandmother. She dragged her rosary across my arms and forehead to put me to sleep. With her love I was safe again but not so trusting of others.

The Convent

Mother took me to school in St. Charles, a small town on the Mississippi River near St. Louis. The whole town seemed to be part of the river, from the cobblestone dock to the brick streets. I felt that it was a very old place.

On the second street from the river stood a four-story dark brick building with enormous windows. A tall black wrought iron fence surrounded its grounds. We entered the front door and sat in the reception room. It had dark paneled walls and dark polished wooden floors. Mother talked to an old nun. They seemed to share many memories. A younger nun asked me to walk down the hall with her. When we returned, no one was in the room. I asked her where Mother was. The nun said she had left. I felt the same shock I remembered when seeing my woods destroyed. My world had changed again. I spent the next four days numb, alone in the convent with nuns.

Finally, the other girls arrived. They had been in the school for years and did not seem bothered by the fence or the routine. Bells signaled all our activities. Nuns rang them by ropes hanging from the dark hall ceiling on the first floor.

The 5:00 a.m. bell meant we carried our pitchers across the hall from our alcoves to a gray bathroom and filled them with water. Then we returned to our bedroom alcoves, washed our faces and hands, and put on our uniforms. We went down the stairs, down the hall, down more stairs, and out the back door to the chapel. It had little balconies in the walls on each side. These were for nuns who sang in high voices at certain times during prayers and masses. I looked up and wondered how they ever got into those places. We knelt on hard boards until six o'clock, then walked to breakfast.

The kitchen and the student dining room were in the basement. The whole convent must have been built on a hill, because the basement in the back was underground, but its north end had the glass doors we entered. We ate at round tables that seated five. The first time I saw the coffee they served, I wondered what it was. I tasted tan milk with very little coffee. I could not make them understand that I wanted it black. A lost cause.

Then we went to the first floor, which had the reception room, small guest rooms, and a large dining room for dignitaries. One hall led to a dark wooden staircase up to long halls and many classrooms. The next floor held our dormitories, which were also dark wood-paneled rooms. Each had alcoves for eight beds, four on one side and four on the other, all separated by white curtains on metal poles. Our only real wall was at the head of the bed. Each girl had a small washstand with a drawer and a large white bowl holding a pitcher. Every afternoon we used soap and water to clean our washstands and beds. A nearby streetcar factory made so much soot that we also changed our shirts twice a day.

Before dinner every evening we were allowed to walk on the grounds west of the building. Because two girls could not walk alone, at least three walked together. We went down a wide sidewalk leading to large trees. Among them was a stone structure built like an outdoor shed, except it was arched and made into a cave. This was called the grotto, a holy place of miracles that held a statue of the Virgin Mary. Beyond the large trees was a space where we played ball on Saturdays.

Saturday evenings we went downstairs to a large room with bathtubs all around the walls. Each was enclosed with the partitions public restrooms have. First we went into a nearby room and took off our shirts. Then the nuns put white capes over us and tied them at our necks before we finished undressing. That was to keep us from being nude or looking at our bodies at any time. A funny sight, I thought—all of us in capes getting into enclosed bathtubs.

My tub was quite large. When I reached for my soap, it fell on the floor and slid under the partition to Betty's tub. I climbed out, got down on the floor, and reached under to find my soap. I heard the nun's clacker. She opened my door and told me I had lost my *tres bien* for the week.

"What is that?" I asked.

It meant when you made the slightest mistake, you were punished by wearing black gloves to Mass on Sunday, instead of white. That showed everyone you were a bad person.

When Sunday came, we entered the church in our usual long procession, with our hands clasped in front of us. Mine were different.

I was enrolled in classes for piano, embroidery, and beginner's Latin. I had not been allowed to bring my paints, so I asked about an art class. They did not have one.

Grandmother had given me a diary so I could write stories about the school for her. I left it in my trunk, which was kept on the very top floor, or attic. That was a long, cold, dark, dreary space with light entering only from windows on the western sloped walls. I opened my trunk, pulled on the bottom drawer, and took out the diary. I wrote that I felt like Dempsey, her canary, in a cage.

Before leaving the attic, I noticed a door partly opened. I tiptoed over and saw three old nuns sitting in rocking chairs facing the windows. The sunlight made a rosary in the first one's hands sparkle like my sisters' diamonds. That nun was asleep with her jaw down on her chest. I could not clearly see the other two. Behind the chairs on the other side of the room were narrow beds. Above each, a black cross.

One week we were told to go to the grotto and assist people who came there every fall to pray for a miracle. The convent was believed to be a place of miracles because of a beloved nun who had been buried years ago in their cemetery. When caskets from that cemetery were moved to one in front of the convent, hers had only water in it, no body. That news went to Rome, and years later she was made a saint. They built a mausoleum for her by the front entrance. The whole place did not seem to be in the real world.

I walked down there with Betty and Maria. A large crowd of old people, deformed people, and people in wheelchairs chanted a litany led by an aged priest. I stood horrified. Then a little girl near me held out her arm, and I saw a hand where her elbow should have been. I turned away and started running.

When I stopped running, I was in the hall by the visitors' rooms. I hid behind a doorway when I heard someone walking toward me. It was the nun to pull the bell rope for chapel. When the other girls came in, I followed them. No one had missed me.

One Friday during breakfast, Maria leaned over the table to say something quietly. We all leaned in to hear, "Let's have a party!" Then we sat back, looking at each other with great interest. She said her father owned delicatessens in St. Louis, so she could get wine and cheese. Betty said she could bring breads. They usually went home on weekends. I had to stay, but I was not so lonely that weekend because of the party.

When Maria returned Sunday, she told the nun in charge of our room that her mother had given her a bottle of tonic. Betty whispered that the cheese was under her mattress near the pillow. Our great secret sparkled in our eyes.

After evening prayers we went to our beds. The nun who sat in the middle of the room waited for us to go to sleep. Then she checked each girl before leaving. Silence. One by one, barefoot, we entered Maria's alcove and climbed on her bed. She passed the bottle. We all drank wine and ate bread and cheese. We giggled and whispered. The wine made us forget to be silent.

Maria said, "Quiet! Listen! I heard a noise."

We looked at each other and knew what it was—retarded Katie. We had forgotten about fat, sloppy Katie. She slept at one end of our room and had been there most of her life. Everyone was afraid of her because they said she was very strong.

"She will tell on us," Betty said.

We heard her floppy shoes approaching. Then I saw them under the curtain. The wine had made me brave, so I pulled the curtain back, jumped forward, and pushed her away. She fell. I stood above her and shook my fist. I put a finger on my mouth to tell her to be quiet. Then I pointed to her bed. I was used to gesturing with Sonny, so it seemed natural. She got up, shook her head back and forth, and returned to her bed. The party continued until the wine was gone. Katie never told on us. She thought I was her friend.

I had very little time to write in my diary. But I managed to tell Grandmother all about the party. I knew she would love it. I closed by saying I would write again after the wiener roast the nuns had planned for Friday night.

Late that Friday when everyone had gone outside, I went to the attic for my diary. It was not there. I knew the nuns were reading about our secret party. I had betrayed my friends by writing in that stupid book. What could I tell them? I had to escape.

I went outside and stood under the trees that were now surrounded by lanterns. Nuns had put coals in a large iron stand that had a boxed top with rods in it. Some of the girls walked around, and others stood by the tables, talking to nuns. I saw Betty and Maria sitting on the ground, and joined them. We watched the lanterns make shadows across us.

Suddenly we heard a girl scream.

"Look!" Betty said, pointing toward the building. A large fiery ball came across the convent roof. Like a basketball, it bounced three times then rolled toward the side and disappeared. We were fascinated. More girls screamed as we ran toward the side door.

We finished the party in the dining room. The nuns said the light was a sign of God over their convent. I thought about the old nun in the attic room and wondered if she had died.

The next evening after chapel, a nun asked me to follow her. We went into a part of the convent I had never seen. She opened a door and told me to enter. In the golden glow of sunset I saw a nun sitting behind a large carved desk. The shelves behind her were full of books. The other walls held pictures, and this floor had a rug.

The nun, in a loud voice, began telling me of my evil ways. I saw my diary on the desk, along with a book Mike had given me, *Utopia*. I had not read it. She asked if I knew why we were put on earth. I had no idea. I just stood there. She asked again, and I still did not have an answer. She came from behind the desk, shook me, and said, "We are here to serve God." She told me I would have to come to her every night so she could make me understand that I had sinned.

So I went there another night. She asked what I had read. I told her and added some books that Mike had read parts of to me—*Brann the Iconoclast* and Balzac's novels. In the middle of my sentence, she slapped me. I was so stunned that I walked to the door and left.

Before dawn the next morning, I took my clothes out of a metal locker, dressed, carried my shoes, slipped out the side door, and ran north to the cemetery. I knew there was a pasture beyond that and hoped I would find a road. It was just light when I saw the river. I crawled between some crates and sat there all morning, shaking and frightened. I could hear water lap against the shore when a boat passed. I had loved the sound of riverboats when I heard their foghorns at night. I finally crawled out because I was hungry. Now I could watch the boats and the wonderful river.

I walked along the main street to the town. When I was by a drugstore, the smell reminded me of the drugstores at home and in Lebanon. I found a table in the back and told the man I wanted a chocolate soda. While I waited, girls from the college came in. They were so carefree.

After they left, I walked around town. When I saw a sign that said "Doctor," I decided to call Pawnee. She and Mike had moved from Ohio to the little house, so she could take me home. I stepped past a woman on her knees scrubbing cobblestones and entered. I saw a telephone on the desk where an old man sat. I said, "Excuse me, sir. Could I use your telephone?"

"Tell me all about it and I will help you use it."

He motioned to a chair near him. I sat down and cried. He called Pawnee. She said she would leave immediately and be there the next afternoon. Then he called the convent, telling them I would return and my sister would pick me up tomorrow.

I walked back. When I entered and looked down the long dark hall, I saw nuns standing on both sides. I walked between them, and the last one took me to a room I had never seen. I waited there, alone, without food.

The next day I was taken to a very pretty bedroom where my sister sat with an older nun. They were whispering and giggling about something that happened long ago. We slept there that night, and the next day the nuns said their farewells at the front door.

Later in the day, Pawnee said, "Jinsey, I am tired. Can you steer this car?" I got behind the wheel and drove many miles across Missouri. Along the way we stopped to get gas. And we found a nice place where travelers could spend the night, a hotel on the highway.

After a long rest, we drove again. In late afternoon on a lovely fall day, we found a small-town drugstore. There was the marble counter with the marble-topped handles that controlled cola and fizz water. We ordered cherry Cokes, pimento cheese sandwiches, and sodas. Pawnee found a box of chocolates to take with us.

Dusk came in deep blues and grays, and soon a large orange moon rose from the flat prairie. We drove the little sedan down the highway, eating chocolates in moonlight.

The Prodigal's Return

We arrived at the little house very tired. Mike was waiting and brought in our grips. He made coffee, and we sat in their small living room to talk about the trip and the convent. Then he said he had something to tell me: I could not go home because Mother was so angry with me. I did not understand.

He said he did not know why she took me out of a good school and sent me to a convent. I looked at Pawnee, who motioned for me to sit by her on the piano bench.

Mike continued, "You will stay with us and out of school for the rest of this year. We will try to educate you."

I felt more confused. When he asked me to say something, I muttered, "It was not my fault."

"What was not your fault?"

So I told them what happened in the closet. We sat silently until Mike said, "That son of a bitch."

Pawnee put her arms around me. Mike kept saying those words Billy had told us men used when they were mad.

The happiest part of my life was then spent with them. We always went to a cafeteria for dinner. Afterward I sat on the floor near his chair and reported about the books he had given me to read. And we talked, and he read to me. This world of new books created new ideas to explore. And the trips we took were always adventures.

Mike was working for the *Tulsa Tribune* newspaper. One of the stories he wrote was about Belle Starr. He said once she was sitting on her horse when she dropped her hat. She said to the man standing by, "Damn it, when a lady drops her hat, pick it up." To learn more about her, we visited Inola and other places she had lived. After that, he became intrigued with western history and began writing about Oklahoma history.

Late one summer morning, we left in the old Winton touring car with its yellow wooden wheels and black canvas top. It had a brass-trimmed horn outside. When you pushed a small button on the driver's side door, the horn said, "Ah-ooga, ah-ooga." The three of us sat on the wide leather front seat. Pauline wore a scarf around her head, and Mike called her Isadora Duncan.

We drove by a town named Keystone by a river named Cimarron, where white birds sat in long rows on rust-colored sandbars. We crossed a single-lane wooden bridge to a rock bluff that went uphill then led to another hill with a view of the valley below. For a few miles we followed this winding road up and down over small hills and curves until we reached the town of Cleveland. Mike called it Grover's Place for the former president.

Sandstone buildings and wood storefronts faced each other across the wide brick street. We stopped at a gasoline pump. Mike asked the man there if he knew of anything interesting going on. He also asked about restrooms. They were behind the building. We went back to find only an outhouse. When we returned, the man said, "Now be sure and go thataway." He pointed toward the west. "There is a homecoming at Pawnee, and if you go thataway you will get to it."

When we drove off, Mike said, "We are now going thataway."

He began to sing, and we sang with him. We stopped to eat a picnic lunch overlooking a small stream where long-legged birds waded. After resting on a quilt, we began our quest to see a homecoming. It was a long time before we reached Pawnee, twenty miles away. It had a square court-house and park in its center, with benches where Indians sat. Streets and buildings were around its four sides. This was a totally new scene. Mike went into a place called a trading post and asked directions. They said to go a few miles to the west. We drove until we saw teepees like the ones in history books. Now they were on each side of road as far as I could see. We drove between them until we came to a long log building with a sign that said "Pawnee Bill's Trading Post."

The porch was made of logs and had a sandstone floor that ran the whole length of the building. A stagecoach sat beside it. Mike pushed open the large wooden door, and we entered a room with a long mahogany bar and shiny brass rails. Behind the bar hung a long mirror with scrolls and a painting of a woman reclining on a Victorian couch. She wore a low-necked red dress and black lace-up boots. One leg was exposed to the knee, showing black lace under her dress. Near the bar were faded old pictures of soldiers on horses.

I began to walk around by myself looking at other photographs of dark Indians and white scouts. They were sitting or standing, staring at the camera. They wore buckskins, beaded shirts, armbands, and moccasins. The Indian men wore headdresses, and the white scouts wore large hats. They held guns or bows and arrows. Some posed in front of a dead bear. Above the photographs, skins of wolves, bobcats, and bears hung from ledges.

Mike and Pawnee motioned me to follow them. We walked into another room that had a large wood-burning fireplace on its west side. A Navaho blanket hung above the fireplace with guns racked across it. In front of the fireplace I saw a man with long white hair and a white mustache. He wore a blue dress suit and cowboy boots. Stepping forward to greet us, he put his arm around me, and I looked up into his blue eyes.

"I am Pawnee Bill," he said. When Mike introduced us, Pawnee Bill insisted we stay for some dances. He took us out in back of the building, waved at a man, and told us to go sit in the brush arbor.

I could smell smoke from campfires. All around us were tall dark-skinned men in clothes of skins, beads, and feathers. They wore short breechcloths and feathered shields on their backs. Some wore beaded armbands. They moved their feet up and down in short staccato movements, then they spun around and looked down at the earth. We were enchanted.

The young girls wore white buckskin with fringes. They stepped side-ways in a two-step movement. Their dresses swayed in unison as they moved in a circle. Some of the women wore dark blue woolen dresses with elk teeth sewn on them. In the center of this ring of dancers, men sat on small stools around a large drum hung in a frame. They beat it and sang a song for each dance. Older women trilled in a high pitch after some of the dances. They wore embroidered shawls, and my sister wanted one. I wanted to walk among the Indians.

We left Pawnee Bill's late in the afternoon and talked about it all the way to Ponca City, where we stayed in a small hotel. Our rooms had coiled ropes at each window. "What is this for?" I asked.

Mike explained, "In case of fire you grab the rope, climb out the window, and slide down it."

The next morning we ate in the hotel restaurant. The counter held a large ham, a pork roast, and glass-covered pies and sweet rolls.

"What will you have, a short stack?" the waitress asked me. I looked at Mike because I did not know what a stack was.

"Yes," he said, grinning. "We will all have a stack."

We were soon served pancakes the size of our plates, with a bowl of butter and a jug of syrup. Pawnee ate the center out of hers, and I managed one. The coffee was wonderful. We sat there laughing about everything. We went back to our rooms and gathered our kits, as Pawnee called our luggage, then drove down a long narrow road to the south of town.

Mike told us we would soon see the 101 Ranch and the house the Millers lived in. He said, "The place will not be like it used to be, but you will sense the romance of it all."

There was a beautiful white house with trees in front–a massive structure of wealth on the prairie. South of it stood a large two-story white building with arched pillars. That was the store. Behind it was where the barns had been. Across the road were grandstands for shows. Round platforms where elephants had done tricks now had bluestem grass growing around them. Beyond them was a pig sty, with pigs running around in a fenced area.

We did not go that far but walked back to the store. A large cage by the door held a bear.

"You can feed him if you want to," said an old man sitting on a nearby box. Mike bought an orange soda, handed it to me, and I gave it to the man. The bear groaned, stood up, took the bottle in his paws, and drank it.

The old man said, "One time me and the boys got the bear drunk and put it in Mrs. Miller's bed."

He laughed, shook his head, and held out his hand to Mike. "My name is Cousin Willie Brooks. The show is on tour at this time." He told us about the cattle barns, horses, wheat fields, and ice houses that were gone now.

Once the ranch even had its own money. He added, "Back there, in that cook shack, we make applejack."

We told him we liked the ranch name. "Well, when Colonel Miller had a small spread, he took the name he wanted for his place to a blacksmith and told him he wanted it to be Bar O Bar. When the brand was put on the cow, like they used to brand, the bar did not turn sideways, so it said 101. The Colonel liked it."

We had wonderful trips in our Winton touring car.

At home, Mike made friends with Frank, a neighbor who worked at the refinery. One evening as Pawnee and Mike and I sat in the cafeteria, Pawnee asked Mike how he had met Frank. Mike told us he had done a newspaper story on all the people from England and France who lived in Tulsa. "I did not realize at the time that he was our neighbor," he said. That's how the tennis court began.

They arranged to build it on the newly cleared land near the school. It was a standard court with high cyclone-fence backdrops. I was allowed to operate a chalk-filled roller to section the court. When it was finished, Mike and Frank played, and I retrieved balls.

One day Mike said, "Here is an old racket of mine. You can have it." I was thrilled. He showed me how to hold it and hit the ball. After they went home, I stayed and slammed balls until I thought I could try to play with Pawnee.

Frank brought his wife, Iza, and daughter, Nadine, to the court one day. After we were introduced, I realized that I used to run through their driveway to visit the barn. I told them I thought their violets were beautiful. Nadine was rather tall, with short, light brown hair. She did not dress up like other girls her age. Iza was very English. She had red hair, blue eyes, and a beautiful figure. Before they left, she said to me, "Dear girl, come for high tea."

Nadine seemed bashful, but she said, "I have a guinea pig. You can hold him."

I was nervous about going to a strange house by myself, but Pawnee picked out a dress for me and said I would enjoy the visit. So I walked across the street at four, and when Nadine opened the door I was so glad I had accepted. The house was filled with old English furniture, Oriental rugs, flowered chintz curtains, and books. I felt at home. Nadine took me to the basement and introduced me to her other friend, the guinea pig.

When we returned upstairs, the four of us sat around a gateleg table with cups and saucers and a teapot in a cozy. Iza brought a tray with cream and sugar and lemon slices. Frank put orange marmalade and tea biscuits beside the pot and carried the tray away. I watched them put sugar and cream or lemon in their tea. Mine was dark in the cup.

Nadine said, "You must put cream and sugar or lemon in it and be English like us."

I became part of their lives for many years.

I was always glad when Sonny came home from school on a break. When the four of us returned from dinner one evening, Lena was waiting on the garage steps. She said, "Miz Jane, Miz Goings wants you to come by in the morning."

"Why does Grandmother want to see me?"

"Nothing wrong. She is fair to middlin' and needs more caring now."

"How can we manage it?"

"Miz Sheppard is going to be out all the morning."

The next morning I waited by the window and watched Mother drive away. Then I ran over to the kitchen and helped Lena carry the breakfast trays upstairs. Grandmother was sitting up in bed. I put her tray on her lap and raised the cover over her hot railroad biscuits and bowl of sorghum with floating butter. I sat beside her and ate the same thing. Lena poured our black coffee. Grandmother reached out to me and we held hands.

I said, "Things can never be the same." I looked at the floor because I did not want Grandmother to see how bad I felt. "Things will never be right again."

She found her handkerchief under her pillow and pressed it to her eyes. "Sending you away was a big mistake. I am appalled by all of this."

I told her the whole story about the convent. She looked at the bedspread, and folded and unfolded her hands. When I finished, she told me that I had her temperament. She explained that Father had wanted all his daughters educated in convents. Part of Mother's anger was that she had spent so much to send me there, "more than we could afford." Finally she said, "I forgive you for leaving, but Lit is very upset about Pauline's bringing you home."

Grandmother nodded toward the door. Lena was sticking her hand through the opening. We both smiled, and I reached over and pulled her into the room. We began laughing, and Lena helped her out of bed. I selected a dress for her then took the cover off the canary cage. Dempsey began singing as I brushed Grandmother's hair. Lena took the trays but soon returned to tell me it was time to leave.

I went out the back door of my house toward the little house. Sonny came running across the yard and pulled me the rest of the way. He had been playing with his Erector set when his little black dog swallowed a part. Pawnee put the dog in her car and we drove to the veterinarian. The dog died.

We were so sad. Pawnee stopped the car by the river. We walked down to the sandy bank and watched the brown water flow. Sometimes leaves or a log drifted along. When I pointed to them, Sonny looked at me with tears in his eyes. As the afternoon began having longer shadows, we returned to the little house. Pawnee said a letter had come for Mike from his sister Kate in New York. We wondered what it said but waited for him to open it.

The letter said Kate's son Tony was coming to visit us next week, before he went to Europe. Mike told me to take it to Mother the next morning. He thought this might help change my situation. I was not sure about what to say, but I went over to the kitchen with the letter. Mother was mixing dough with her hands.

"I brought a letter for you to read." Silence. "This is important. We want you to read it." She kept mixing the dough, but suddenly the dough was in my face. I ran out the back door to Pawnee. She held me, dough and all. Then she called Mike at the *Tribune*. He said he would go see Mother that evening. After Mike talked to her, it was all arranged. Tony would stay in the best front bedroom, and we would act like a loving family.

Two days later, Mike, Pawnee, Sonny, and I drove to the station. As we stood waiting, men pushed large rattling green wagons toward the tracks for unloading boxes and packages. The big train engine roared in, shaking the ground. Then it was in front of us, hissing and clinking as it stopped.

I saw a rather tall boy with blond hair jump over the box a porter had put there for people to step on. "That is Tony," Mike said. We walked over to him, and he put his arms around all of us. He called me "Cousin." Sonny tugged at my arm and pointed to Tony's blond hair.

Tony became the center of our lives for a week. He told us he loved our house and the country he saw from the train. He talked to us about everything. Mother told Lena to serve him breakfast in bed. We ate dinner in the dining room and sat around the table afterward talking about family and sports. Again, Mike mentioned Notre Dame.

Mike had hoped the weather would be nice for tennis, and it was. I told Nadine about Tony, so she came to the court with Frank. She and I sat together as she watched every move Tony made. She whispered, "Oh, his hair is like sunshine. Oh, isn't he wonderful?"

Well, I thought he was a lot of fun and very smart, but I did not think he was wonderful. Nadine watched him play tennis every day.

After Tony left, a friend of Pawnee's stopped by. Marguerite Parker was twenty-five, tall, with light brown hair, gray eyes, and a curved nose that gave her a dignified look. She had been in Vienna for a year taking art classes. Pawnee insisted that she spend the winter with us. Mother liked her and had the carpenters fix up the attic into a studio. Marguerite gave me art lessons there. We painted old vases with berries in them and other table arrangements. We walked along the river and made pen and ink sketches of the refinery, then watercolor washes of the bridge. Pawnee had all my artwork framed.

It was a happy time for me. Then Marguerite's mother wrote that she should come home and find someone to marry. We did not want her to leave.

Mother finally decided I could move back into our house. I was glad. I felt so comfortable there. I loved to sit in the dining room at sunset and watch the colors change. I found the library books more interesting than ever and spent lots of time reading.

New Beginnings

One evening after dinner, Mother said she had received a telegram from Edwina. It said Pep had died of pneumonia in Chicago. Edwina was going to Champaign to get a coal royalty from his mother. We were silent until Mother added, "After that she is coming to Tulsa."

I had nothing to say. Mother told me I must be very kind to the boys.

Edwina found a large white house down on Main near the drugstore. I went over there once with Mother. It was a pretty place. She had all of Father's office furniture. I wondered how she got it but did not ask. I loved the Morris chair and other designs of the time. She had added more furniture and soaked some of the chairs in a lye solution to remove paint.

I was told I had to teach Billy to dance so he could escort me to the Pattens' dinner party. So I began the tedious task of teaching him to move one leg, then the other. "One, two," I would say.

The night of the party, Billy wore a dark suit, and I wore light blue taffeta and velvet. We walked up the block and a half and saw colorful reflections of car lights on other arriving guests. The living room was filled with boys and girls standing and sitting in groups, talking and laughing.

When dinner was announced, we were seated at a beautiful table of gold service with a rose at each plate. The boys gave their roses to the girls next to them. Everyone began to realize that this was a serious moment. We were in training for the rest of our lives. We watched the hostess for cues. Billy was quiet for a change and very polite to the girl beside him. Later he whispered to me that he thought she was ugly.

Joe and Nick took Perry out of his wheelchair for the evening, so he would be like the rest of us. Tall, redheaded Tom Yancy danced with Nadine.

Most of the girls I knew were there, except for one who lived in the old O'Conner house. Mother said they rented.

As Billy and I walked home in the dark, we talked about growing up. Billy said he was going to be a writer, then he could do what he pleased. I said I was going to be an artist. The door to our house opened, and Pawnee took me upstairs and put me to bed. Mother hugged Billy and told him he would sleep on the daybed in the breakfast room.

It was a lovely evening.

Mike enrolled me in the public high school downtown and drove me there every morning. I went up Central's wide white marble steps into a long hall full of boys and girls my age and older walking around and going in and out of rooms. They wore all sorts of clothes. I was used to a small girls' school where we wore uniforms. I had a card with a list of classes but did not know where to go. I panicked. I walked in the first door on the right and talked to the woman there. She told me where to go and that I would have two classes with her later in the day. She taught botany and biology.

I told Pawnee and Mike about all my classes and some of the girls I met. Three of them drove me home the second week. One kept calling me at night until Mike put a stop to it. He said he had to explain things to me. I began to awaken to what happened around me at school. The boys and girls went together, and they had special meeting places in the halls. I felt my other self was still at home playing basketball, while my new self was in this world of new experiences.

One morning when I was in a class, Mike entered the room. The young teacher motioned for me to go into the hall. I waited while he talked to her. They talked a long time. Then he came out smiling and said, "Well, the old girl finally kicked the bucket. It was about time."

"What are you talking about?" I asked as we walked down the hall.

"She was sitting up in bed with her breakfast tray and she just fell over."

Then I knew it was my grandmother. I began to sob, but he kept smiling. A deep resentment came over me. My dear grandmother. How could this be. After he drove me home, I went up to her room. Mother and Wells were digging through her trunk. Oh, Grandmother, you would not like that, I said to myself.

I went downstairs to see Lena. She was running the large gas-fired mangle, watching a sheet roll through. I waited until that one was finished. Then I asked where they took Grandmother.

"She be at the place up by the church. The angels done took that sweet lady."

I went out the basement door and started walking up Cheyenne. At the funeral home I went into the room where I saw her casket. She was so small and looked so white. I stood by her a long time, then told her I had come to see her. I cried. Mother and Wells came. I left.

I was glad I had gone to see her and told her goodbye. They did not invite me to her funeral. No one put a headstone on her grave. I do not know what happened to her things except for the furniture Wells took, but I will always remember the postcard of the bear with real black fur.

I wished someone had told me about Grandmother's life. I knew her name was Tennessee because when she taught me spelling, she had me spell it. Though I felt close to her son Uncle B.B., when Uncle Will came to visit I was not able to talk with him much. He brought Mother a large black grip full of dahlias he had grown. I wanted to hold them. Grandmother's third son, a doctor, had died of pneumonia before we came to Oklahoma.

I was very lonely after that. I wanted someone to hear how much I missed her. But our family just did not talk about how we felt. It would always be this way. So I kept my grief all to myself in the day and cried alone at night. Mother probably did the same.

The constant routine at Central High became the biggest part of my life. I especially enjoyed the art class taught by Mrs. Corrubia because she spoke to me about art and what she would like me to do. I painted large signs for her. At last I could do something with paints and brushes. The time I spent there seemed to help my loneliness.

One afternoon while I worked on a large sign, Mrs. Corrubia introduced me to a boy named Martin Gardner. He was rather tall and thin, with very dark eyes. He talked constantly about science and theories while I painted. Then he stopped, looked at me, and said, "Why are you wearing that jewelry?"

I had a necklace of blue, yellow, and plain wooden beads. I told him my sister had given it to me. He said, "Those are material things, and useless. You must come with the Corrubias to my house and meet people who have intelligent conversations about things of importance."

So it was arranged that instead of going to the school Daze program, I would go to Martin's house. I was introduced to doctors, laborers, and businessmen. I felt unsure of myself with all those adults, so I remained silent and listened. They talked about China and how we should help. They called each other "comrade." They talked about needing people in schools, factories, and corporations. They said one person who knew how to work a crowd could make the change. I was introduced to the head of the Communist party in America. He had come west to recruit people.

I wondered why a boy who lived on this beautiful estate and had everything would be interested in something like Communism. I had spent most of a year listening to Mike talk about characters in books and real people in newspaper stories. Talking to Mike and Pawnee about this meeting would have been interesting, but of course I could not because I might get sent away again.

For the next meeting, my teacher came by, and we drove east of town to a rambling two-story white house on a large farm. We went into a kitchen lined with sideboards. The center had a long plain wooden table surrounded by chairs. The house had many rooms for visitors, and the bathrooms had sewing machines in their alcoves. People who lived there said they canned, made bread, and cured their own meat. When children came home from school, they dropped their books and took buckets to the field to gather vegetables. Everyone worked. I was amazed by the easy way they lived and cared for others.

Martin explained, "This is called socialism. This is another organization trying to change the capitalistic world."

One afternoon Martin came by our house to borrow a book by Ingersoll. I knew he would take good care of it. Later that week, Mother called me into the living room and asked me to explain how I could loan one of her books to that boy. I asked why it was so important, as he said he would return it.

"He certainly will! His father called me very angry. He had come home from Europe and found his son reading a book by an atheist."

When Martin returned the book, he brought another one with him. He said, "I am going to conduct an experiment. I will read out of my book, and you are supposed to listen, then jump up out of your chair, raise your arms, and say 'God is making me whole.'"

So he read it, and I jumped out of my chair and said, "God is making me whole," with my arms out in a ballet position.

"Do you feel any different?" he asked.

"No. How am I supposed to feel?"

Martin put the book down and said, "You are supposed to be saved."

I dropped my arms, sat down, and said, "Saved from what?" He told me that this experiment was not successful. It could not be proved and therefore was not a fact. I told Mike and Pawnee about it that evening, and Mike said Martin would grow up to be a scientist.

Mike told us he had bought the Plaza Theater out at Fifteenth and Peoria. Pawnee said, "Oh, just think! We can have all the movie stars in our own place!"

We went to see a matinee, then went again at midnight to screen films. Mike said he was going to change many things, first the signs outside and in the lobby. He had an artist in mind, E. Albin. Mike said he wanted me to spend Saturdays with the artist. Mrs. Corrubia had taught me to paint special effects, so I felt confident.

The next Saturday while I stood in the lobby waiting for Mr. Albin, I started talking to two boys waiting to see Mike. They asked if I planned to work there. I told them I would fill in signs. The taller boy introduced himself as Bill Goldrich and his friend as Ed Flaherty. They hoped to be ushers.

Then he said, "You are the girl I am going to marry."

I just looked at him. Mike was walking toward us, so I said I had to go.

The next day at school I was surprised to see Bill walking down the hall with a girl. What a relief when he introduced his sister Lucille. They asked if I would come to their house after school. I hesitated but thought about how I stood on the corner waiting for a bus, looking at the dark red brick Springer Clinic where sick people went. I decided to accept their offer.

We drove out Peoria and around a corner to their two-story brick house. All the houses there were new and had beautiful yards. I met his mother and other sister. They said they were from New York and could trace their ancestry to the *Mayflower.* I could only say we came from West Virginia. I watched the mother and daughter do needlepoint while the boys went to their garage to work on a glider. Being with them was fun.

Sketch by Jane

Every Saturday evening, Bill and Ed and I drove their Model A to town and went up and down Main, over and over. It was a fiesta of cars with people waving, honking, and touching hands. Every time we passed someone, we greeted them again. One fellow had a Cord, another a Rolls Royce, another a Packard, and Jack had a Franklin.

And there was always Max, our Jewish friend, in his grandfather's very old sedan. Grandfather, with his long white beard, was usually in the back seat. Once we went to their magnificent home. They had large mahogany tables covered with statues. They had European tapestries and furniture. Their garage held four cars. One Saturday night Max was told he had to pick up Grandfather and an old goat at the train station. We thought the goat would be a grumpy old person. But that night Max drove up and down Main with Grandfather and a real live goat in the back seat.

At home I usually studied with Pawnee and Mike. Then Edwina started coming nearly every night. She seemed to spend most of her time at our house or the little house. When I went there with my books, she would say, "Why don't you go home. We are busy." Then I studied in our dining room. I missed them.

One Sunday Bill came over in a Model T. It was the funniest car I had ever seen. He said he was going to design a new set of gears for it. Now he wanted to try it down Riverside Drive, as the road had been extended to Quicksand Creek. He could turn around by the Chinese celery farm.

When we returned, Lena said Mike was looking for us. As we waited for him, Bill stood by the living room fireplace, and I sat on the couch. Mike walked in and stood by Bill. He said, "Young man, I do not need your services any longer, and your relationship with my niece is over."

Bill politely said, "Yes, sir. I understand you, sir."

I was shocked.

"You heard what I said," Mike told me as he left the room. Bill sat beside me and held my hand. We looked at each other and knew we would work something out.

When I told Pawnee what had happened, she said Mike and Edwina thought I should find a wealthy man instead of a boy. "I don't want anything of the sort," I replied. I asked, "Why is he listening to Edwina? She just wants to run other people's lives." I remembered when she took my father away.

Mike picked a man named John Strayhorn to take me on a date. We went to a movie, then he asked if I would like a soda. I shook my head. I was furious about the whole thing. John said he would like to talk to me. I agreed.

He said, "Jane, I feel awkward with you because you are so young."

I answered, "John, I am very sorry about this. I did not want to go out with you." He understood. We enjoyed our sodas as he talked about his work and his life. We never saw each other again.

Bill and I continued meeting. We left Central in different ways instead of together. One time at a side door I saw the young teacher that Mike had talked to get into Mike's car. But I could not say anything about it.

Bill's mother wanted all his friends to come over one Sunday for lunch. Bill had rebuilt his Model T, and he was going to try it out on Saturday. She was sure it would be a success to celebrate. Faye said she would pick me up and everyone would think we were going to her house.

That Saturday afternoon, Lena told me my friend Ed was waiting in the living room. When he looked at me, I asked, "What's wrong?"

He told me that when Bill drove his little car around the block, another car ran into him at a corner, killing him instantly. We sat on the couch without talking. Lena came in and saw how upset we were, so she brought us hot coffee. We stayed there a long time. After he left, I felt so alone. I tried telling Mother, but she did not seem to care. I could not talk to Mike and Pawnee about him. No one told me to send flowers. No one took me to the funeral.

Ed came back after it was over, and we spent a lot of time together. Then Jack, the boy who drove the Franklin, was killed in a wreck. He had been going with Bill's sister Lucille. And when M.K. was driving her new roadster, a car ran into her. The rest of us seemed to lose interest in being together.

One summer day Father's former bookkeeper, Duncan Sanford, came to our house. A few minutes after that, Roy entered our garage in the limousine he drove for the Travis family. They both went into the living room. Mother and Pawnee came in from the door near the little house and also went to the living room. Pawnee was crying.

Looking for Lena, I went to the kitchen, then the basement. She was lying on her bed. I asked, "Lena, why is Roy here? What has happened?"

She sat up and brought the ironing chair over for me. Then she sat on the bed again and said, "Things is real bad." She raised her hands above her head and pressed them together. "Miss Edwina and Mr. Mike is down at the Tulsa Hotel, and they is drunk. The hotel man called Miz Sheppard and told her to come get them."

I could not believe it. But it was true if Lena told me.

"How did they know to call Mother?"

"Yessum, they did, cause they was using Mr. John A.'s name and they knowed it was not him."

This was more than I could understand. I went back up to the center landing of the stairs and sat in the corner with my dolls. Roy and Duncan left together. I watched Pawnee walk through the hall and followed her to the little house. I knew she needed me. She was sitting in Mike's chair when I walked in.

She told me Edwina knew Mike was an alcoholic, so she tricked him into drinking. He had lost his fine job in Ohio because he and his boss were very drunk one night when they were driving home. The boss ran into a construction site. A large piece of wood went through the windshield, killing him instantly. She said she had hoped everything would be different here.

We heard Roy drive into the garage below us. Pawnee told me to slip out the back door. A long time ago I had watched my father eat a peach, then walk out the kitchen door and plant the seed near the little house steps. I went there, thinking I would feel better by his tree. I watched Roy half carry, half drag, a very drunk Mike up the steps. Pawnee opened the door. Then Roy went down to the garage and drove away. When I went back to our house, Mother said Duncan had gone too. I had thought my life would always be the same and Mike would keep me safe. Now I realized again that things would never be the same.

Several days later, I heard Mother talking to Edwina in our breakfast room, telling her to stay away from Pawnee and Mike. I waited in the hall because I wanted to say something to Edwina. I watched her walking defiantly through the dining room.

"Edwina," I began. She stopped. "You should apologize to your sister."

With a wild look in her eyes, she slapped me. "How dare you!" she said. She slapped me again and left, slamming the front door.

After about a week, Pawnee told us Mike was well enough to return to work. The next morning I watched him drive away in the old touring car. That evening I sat on the front porch steps waiting for him. He always drove down the street, turned off the motor, turned right, and then turned left into the garage. This time, he never came back. Jack stayed at our house for a while, but later he and Billy and Mike and Edwina disappeared. We did not know for a long time that they had gone to California.

Now Mother spent even more time with Wells. I knew that Pawnee was heartbroken, and I had to care for her. After about a month, she asked me to go with her to Jenkins for some new sheet music. That Sunday while Mother was at Mass, we went to our big Steinway, and Pawnee began playing jazz. Lena came into the room and stood with arms down by her side. She began to slide one foot and shuffle, then slide the other. Pawnee laughed. Music made us all happy.

After her divorce, Pawnee returned to West Virginia, where she had friends. She married Lathrop O'Keefe and lived there a long time. Sonny continued at the school for the deaf and spent holidays with them.

When I came home from school one day, the room where I watched the sun set across the river was empty. The Adam dining room set from England was gone. Since I was more alone than ever, to be alone without those beautiful things was frightening. There must be some mistake, I thought. I moved quickly through the house trying to find Mother. She was upstairs. I asked her what happened.

"We lost our home," she said. That was all.

"Where is our dining room set?"

"The banker's wife bought it."

I did not know about money or how to use it. I had never been told about our finances. This was hard to understand.

"The vans will come tomorrow. We will move to a house on Frisco."

"This is my home!" I cried. "How can this be happening?"

Our friend Prof said he would help move the paintings and lovely vases. I told him I could not stand this and would not move. He said we must, and when we must do something, it is up to us to do the best we can. The two of us went to the new house and waited for the large paintings. He had a bottle of apricot brandy we drank while waiting. When the movers came, Prof and I tried to hang the pictures straight, but the brandy had created another dimension, and everything was at an angle. We laughed and stumbled around, so I managed to get through the move. I never went back to 1904 South Cheyenne. I was never part of that social scene again. Now we rented.

The new house was small, but Mother made it charming. It had two bedrooms upstairs and a large carpeted game room in the basement, along with a room for Lena and places for trunks. I chose the game room because I could have all my paints and books there.

When Halloween came, I was in my room sprawled on the floor trying to design a poster for school. Prof called down that he was sending someone to meet me. I did not get up. Soon I saw a pair of riding boots. The man seemed interested in what I was doing. He told me had planned to marry a girl who had died. I told him I had been going with a boy who died. Then Prof called him, and he turned to leave.

"What is your name?" he asked.

I told him to call me Jane then asked his name.

"My name is Paul."

I stood up and we looked at each other. I asked, "Did the bird live?"

He often came by with Prof, bringing his friend Hershel. We walked to the library and to Woolworth's on Main Street. Prof loved to go to its basement restaurant for mincemeat pie and coffee with cream and sugar. He introduced me to Ray and Emmett, who owned a dry cleaning shop, and two women who ran a dress shop in their large home on Denver. I drifted into this group. Mother liked them too.

But the house began seeming strange to us. One night Lena awakened me, and I let her into my room. She said, "They is haunts in that trunk room."

I took her upstairs to Mother, and we made a bed for her in front of the living room fireplace. There she said a strong light came across the room. I had a picture of Bill and Ed and their car on my dresser. It moved slightly and fell off. Mother told me that one day when I was at school, a woman came crying and saying this was her house that had been taken away from her. Mother said we had better move. Her mountain heritage and the old stories of haunts made her decide.

Jane 1933

At school I had another set of friends that included the boy named Bill Johnson I had seen at meetings with Martin. Bill started joining our group at the drugstore before school. Ed Flaherty did not seem happy about my interest in Bill, but he went along. He cautioned, though, "He is not like our Bill, and you cannot replace him this way."

Bill Johnson and Jane 1933

Martin had said there would be another meeting on the north side of town. The night he drove me there, we told our parents that we had to be at Central. I was shocked when I saw we were in an industrial area and in a shack without any furniture. Our seats were only wooden boxes, and some Negroes sat among us. The white men looked rough, wearing workers' clothes and old boots. An unsmiling large woman with short brown hair wore the same clothes. She had the fanatical look Mike had told me about one night when we went to a revival meeting. He said, "Watch out. Those people are dangerous."

As my discomfort grew, I asked Martin if he could take me home. He said he had to stay. Bill had come in late and sat on the floor near me. I whispered to him that I would like to leave and asked him to take me home. He said he lived about ten blocks away on Cheyenne, and we could walk there. I told him I had lived on Cheyenne too.

Rain began as we walked down the dark street. When lightning flashed, we saw a house with one window that glowed like a painting. We started there for shelter from the rain and darkness. When we looked inside the window, we saw candles burning and a group of men in a circle. They wore black robes with black hoods over their heads. When one stepped back from the circle, we saw a large white goat in the center of their ceremony.

Bill said, "We had better get away from here and just walk in the rain."

After we crossed a railroad track and turned west toward Cheyenne, we were out of the industrial area. Finally we walked up a driveway to his two-story home.

I heard a piano playing and someone singing. It was his sister. His mother told me they were from West Virginia too, and that Bill was born there in August just a day before me. She was very kind and made us tea. Later he drove me home in his sister's beautiful Auburn car.

At last I felt very safe.

Epilogue

Jane and Bill, and apparently Martin, abandoned their youthful enthusiasm for Communism. Martin became one of America's foremost mathematicians. Jane married Bill and had three children. After they divorced, he moved east to serve in World War II, returning to Tulsa only decades later. Jane's subsequent marriage to Paul lasted until his death. She worked as a floral designer for many years but returned to painting in the 1950s. She entered art shows, won local awards, and sold many paintings. After a third marriage, she also applied her talent to spinning and weaving and restoring oil paintings. Her genealogical research before joining the Daughters of the American Revolution produced valuable information for family members. For many years, she collected Indian art, rugs, pottery, and jewelry. Before her death at ninety-three, she gave part of her collection to museums.

Jane's mother, Lydia, endured further reduced circumstances but kept her favorite Chinese furniture and many other beautiful possessions. She played bridge avidly and wrote her own crossword puzzle dictionary. She sewed for her granddaughters, and she made and sold collectable dolls clothed in luxurious fabrics and leathers from her former wardrobe. Before her final illness, she was writing song lyrics and children's stories. Her loving ten grandchildren called her Muzzy, one of the many family nicknames.

The Sheppard sisters and the entire family finally maintained good relations. Those who did not live in Tulsa kept in contact and visited fairly often.

Edwina, after years in California, returned to West Virginia, built a home, and helped raise and educate several of Pauline and Mike's grandchildren. Her untiring efforts toward restoring family land claims resulted in generous gas and coal royalties for the Sheppard heirs. She established JASMER, an educational, ecological reservation named for John A. For all those efforts she earned a great deal of respect. The JASMER cemetery contains her remains along with those of her sons.

Billy (Curtis G. "Bill" Pepper) and Jack (John Sheppard Pepper) both became journalists after active service in World War II. Jack spent years in Las Vegas then returned to California and published a magazine until his premature death from cancer. Bill remained in Italy after the war, married, and brought up his two children there. He had a successful career in journalism, published a last novel in his nineties, and left a posthumous book on happiness.

After Pauline's second marriage ended, she returned to Tulsa and died fairly young. For many years, Sonny (John Michael Fanning) lived in California, where Mike had become a powerful politician. Sonny and his wife spent their last years in Tulsa with the youngest of their five children.

Wells had a long and successful marriage. The couple remained Lydia's closest companions and constant bridge partners. Their home, complete with four children, was a center of activities—always open and welcoming to everyone.

Roy Green continued being a popular driver, butler, and handyman for Tulsans. Lena, whose last name Jane never knew, probably moved to Texas. Gertrude stayed in Tulsa and sometimes helped Jane.

Both Kenwood and the Buena Vista neighborhood that includes 1904 South Cheyenne are in the National Register of Historic Homes.

Sally Jane, Lydia Jane, and Jane, Downtown Tulsa 1940

Bill Pepper and Jane in their late 80's

CPSIA information can be obtained
at www.ICGtesting.com
Printed in the USA
FSOW02n1150101116
27226FS